CANE TOPPER
Woodcarving

Projects, Patterns, and Essential Techniques for Custom Canes and Walking Sticks

Lora S. Irish

Acknowledgements

I wish to extend my deepest thanks to Chris Reggio, Bud Sperry, Colleen Dorsey, and Christopher Morrison for their excellent work in the creation, development, and refinement of this manuscript. As an author, it is a wonderful experience to be working with such a well-skilled team.

ISBN 978-1-56523-959-3

Library of Congress Cataloging-in-Publication Data

Names: Irish, Lora S., author.
Title: Cane topper woodcarving / Lora S. Irish.
Description: Mount Joy : Fox Chapel Publishing, 2018. | Includes index.
Identifiers: LCCN 2018031758 | ISBN 9781565239593 (pbk.)
Subjects: LCSH: Wood-carving. | Staffs (Sticks, canes, etc.)
Classification: LCC TT199.7 .I7447 2018 | DDC 736/.4--dc23
LC record available at https://lccn.loc.gov/2018031758

To learn more about the other great books from Fox Chapel Publishing, or to find a retailer near you, call toll-free 800-457-9112 or visit us at *www.FoxChapelPublishing.com*.

We are always looking for talented authors. To submit an idea, please send a brief inquiry to acquisitions@foxchapelpublishing.com.

Printed in Singapore
First printing

Because working with wood and other materials inherently includes the risk of injury and damage, this book cannot guarantee that creating the projects in this book is safe for everyone. For this reason, this book is sold without warranties or guarantees of any kind, expressed or implied, and the publisher and the author disclaim any liability for any injuries, losses, or damages caused in any way by the content of this book or the reader's use of the tools needed to complete the projects presented here. The publisher and the author urge all readers to thoroughly review each project and to understand the use of all tools before beginning any project.

Introduction

I love woodcarving. I love the feel of the wood in my hands and the movement of a crisply sharp tool working through the grain. Woodcarving is a hobby that encompasses all forms of designs, themes, and art styles.

But as an avid crafter and hobbyist, I also want an art form that does not take me away from my family. The carving projects that I work are primarily designs that I can create in my home, at my studio table, or in my lap during the evening hours as I join my family around the TV, watching a favorite movie.

Working a decorative carving directly into a 5-foot (155cm)–long walking stick means that I need a large, open space in which to move, turn, and twist the staff. By dividing the cane into small sections—the cane topper, the joint, the joint cover, and the staff—I can carve and construct a cane anywhere and in just about any space, including in the living room or on my back porch.

Working in sections also lets me mix different woods with different assets in one design. I can carve the decorative topper in basswood, which is a fine-grained, white-colored wood that carves easily, and then attach that carving to a hardwood walnut dowel, which will give my stick the strength it needs to act as a hiking stick.

For all these reasons, cane toppers truly give me everything that I want as a woodcarver—the choice of any theme that I can imagine, the ability to work in any location that I want, and the option to incorporate the strongest assets of the woods available to me.

Throughout this book, you will learn how you, too, can take advantage of this fun and rewarding carving genre. I have no doubt that there will be many cozy carving evenings in your future.

Disclaimer

Hand-carved canes, walking sticks, and hiking sticks are meant to be used; they are far more than just decorative items. Throughout this book, we will work together to create our walking sticks with as strong and durable a joint between the cane topper and the staff as possible, which will allow the finished canes to bring decades of joy to their owners.

However, the projects and teachings in this book are not meant in any manner to be a substitute for or to represent a medically necessary walking-assistance device. Anyone who needs a cane for physical support should consult his or her doctor and follow the doctor's recommendations for the specific type and style of cane needed.

Contents

Chapter 1: Staffs

You may not actually carve it, but the staff portion of any cane or walking stick is a very important aspect of the piece. A beautiful, expertly done topper carving doesn't do much good if it isn't serving as the top of something useful! In this section, we will explore the best ways to source and prepare staffs, the various kinds of wood to consider harvesting for staffs, and the many ways you can treat staffs. You'll soon see that there is a world of possibilities out there just to do with staffs.

Harvesting Staffs

Autumn is my favorite time to harvest the year's crop of walking stick wood. The leaves are changing and beginning to fall, which makes finding and identifying the different tree species easier. The sap in the trunks has begun to drop, so the drying time is less than it would be for a spring-cut sapling. But you can harvest at any time during the year, especially if there are downed trees because of storm damage or if you are doing yard work and pruning. Let's look at some tips and ideas for how to harvest, store, and dry walking stick wood.

Harvesting from Your Landscaped Yard

- If you have a landscaped yard, you may have several tree and shrub species that will work wonderfully for walking sticks and canes. Maple, oak, and elm are common landscaping trees that can provide long, straight branches. Winged euonymus (burning bush), rhododendron, crepe myrtle, and bamboo are common yard cultivars that provide great stick material.
- If you are taking prunings, learn how to properly cut the branch and seal the wound to prevent damage and disease to your trees. There are many books and online articles on this subject.
- Storm damage can provide a vast amount of walking stick material, but please make sure you are safe from downed electrical wires before cutting any branches.
- Your local county may have an area set aside for dumping landscaping trimmings at the local landfill. Often you can find great branches there that have been discarded by other homeowners and which are free for the taking.

Harvesting in the Wild/on Others' Property

- Before you begin harvesting along any roadside, open field, or wooded lot, get the permission of the landowner before entering the property. Even if the tree saplings that you want to harvest are on the road side of a fence line, the landowner's property rights extend to the centerline of the road in many jurisdictions. You can avoid a lot of problems by simply asking permission before you cut.
- When you speak with landowners, tell them what you intend to do with the sticks, how many you hope to harvest, and what particular types of trees you want to harvest. I ask the owners for suggestions as to where I might cut on their land and which areas they want me to avoid. Some property owners will allow you to cut specific species but want to protect others from harvest—they may allow you to cut oak, maple, and black locust but not want you to cut any sassafras or dogwood, for example.
- If you harvest wood from someone's lot where you have not cut before, you might want to take along a finished stick as a gift to the owner. A stick in hand is worth 25 or more small saplings, and happy, satisfied landowners will let you harvest on their land year after year.
- Always let someone know where you will be harvesting. Map out the territory and give a time estimate of when you will be returning home. Take your cell phone with you. Accidents can happen, so be prepared!
- Take a small camp shovel with you to dig out the root systems for briar roses, sassafras, and dogwoods. The bulbous root nodes make wonderful stick handles. Remember to backfill any hole that you dig.
- Take along a folding camp saw for branch harvesting. They are lighter to carry than large pruners. Small hand clippers and a good pocketknife are excellent for cleaning the side branches from the main walking stick. Lightweight nylon cord can be used to bundle your sticks and to make a carrying handle to get your harvest back to your car.
- Know the sport hunting laws and timetables for your region. I never harvest after November 1, because in my area that is deer hunting season, which includes bow, black powder, and shotgun. Late September through October 30 is when I do my stick harvesting.

Storage and Drying

When it comes to storage and drying, walking stick carvers tend to have their own personal techniques. If you belong to a carving club or have access to online message boards for your region, take the time to ask your local carvers what works best for them. They know your climate and your tree species, so their advice is well worth discovering.

As a general rule of thumb, fresh-cut wood is dried for one year for each 1" (2.5cm) of thickness. This means that a 4" (10cm) slab of newly cut wood will take about four years to properly dry for woodworking. But since we are working with cut branches that are usually 2" (5cm) or less in diameter, most cut sticks only need about six weeks before they are ready to work as green wood sticks. Because we are cutting our staffs in the fall and winter seasons, the sap content tends to be lower in the tree than it would be during warm weather. Your fall-cut sticks have less sap and moisture that needs to escape from the wood. The moisture also has less wood surface from which to escape, so small-width sticks dry to a working moisture level quicker than larger, thicker sticks. Walking stick saplings cut in the early fall are well ready to work by the beginning of the new year. These green wood–worked sticks will continue to dry over time after you have created your walking stick without affecting your connecting joints.

I bundle my sticks in groups of 10 to 12 using ¼" (0.5cm) nylon rope. The rope is looped around the wide end—the root end—of the stick, with the rope ends tied into a hanging loop. The group is then hung from the rafters of an unheated shed or under the outside roof overhang of the shed. I allow about 6" (15cm) to 8" (20.5cm) of space between groups for air circulation. This keeps the sticks out of direct sunlight and rain.

Common Tree Species

Autumn is the traditional time of the year to harvest tree saplings, branches, and twistie sticks for cane and walking stick carving. As the leaves change color and begin to drop, the branches and trunks of the available saplings become more visible. The sap in the tree's vascular system is dropping, which aids in drying. During one morning's walk through my yard, I found thirteen favorite tree saplings and cultivar branches that could be used in walking stick woodcarving.

Hickory (Carya tomentosa)

This extremely dense hardwood is perfect for small walking sticks and canes. It is commonly used for tool handles, wheel spokes, golf club shafts, and canoe paddles because of its strength. Hickory grows in the eastern half of North America, and is often found in association with oak and maple forests. The sample shown here is actually *Carya cordiformis*, commonly called bitternut hickory, swamp hickory, or pecan hickory. Hickory is a major food source for the luna moth.

Hickory has a medium-gray coloring with light texture. Pale white and light green spotting is common in the older growth areas of the bark. Look along the edge of the wood line and forest for this particular tree.

Black Walnut (Juglans nigra)

Traditionally this hardwood is used for gun stocks, furniture, and flooring, and its nuts are also edible. Walnut hulls have been used to create writing ink and dyes. Growing from the east coast through Midwestern sections of the United States, it was introduced to Europe as a cultivated species in 1629. It is a pioneer species, along with black cherry and silver maple, populating open fields and wetlands in advance of larger forest growth.

Often called weed trees, black walnuts grow quickly. A two-year-old seedling can stand 6 feet (1.8m) to 8 feet (2.4m) tall and have a base diameter of 1½" (3.8cm), the perfect size for a cane stick. The sample shown here is an eastern black walnut, whose highly textured back has a reddish-brown coloration.

English Walnut (Juglans regia)

Also called Persian walnut, white walnut, Old World walnut, and California walnut, these trees are native to the Balkans, eastward into the Himalayas, and in southwest China. Its wide distribution throughout the world is due to its easy cultivation and harvest for its nuts. In the fourth century, English walnut was introduced to Macedonia by Alexander the Great. It has a very smooth, pale gray bark and can attain heights of up to 100 feet (30m). It is used for gun stocks, furniture, guitars, and veneer.

Oak (Quercus *sp.*)

There are approximately 600 extant species of oak, which is a common tree in most of the northern hemisphere. The United States has nearly 90 native species, which are commonly found in large forest stands and in home landscaping. This is major furniture wood and is used in timber-framed buildings and ship construction. Oak bark, rich in tannin, is used in tanning leathers.

The sample shown here is a species of white oak, and happens to be the state tree of Maryland. White oak has a medium-gray coloration with large white spottings. Lichen and moss are often found growing on the branches. The texture of oak changes dramatically depending on the age of the branch. All oak bark has some rough texture, and as the tree ages, the bark develops troughs and ridges that can be up to ½" (1.5cm) in depth.

Oak is an extremely dense hardwood, which gives it the strength needed for quality walking sticks.

However, because oak tends to branch quickly and at a young age, you seldom find long, straight trunks. Note in the sample photo that this four- to five-year-old sapling already has several angles in its main trunk.

Red Cedar (Juniperus virginiana)

Red cedar is not a true cedar, even though that is its common name. Eastern red cedar, pencil cedar, and aromatic cedar are all part of the juniper family. This slow-growing hardwood prefers poor, dry soil conditions and is found throughout the eastern United States. It is a pioneer species, taking root in open fields and surrounding abandoned buildings.

Because of its purple-red heartwood, cedar is often used for decorative woodworking and furniture, such as in cedar chests or cedar closets. At one time, this species was a common fence post wood. Cedar can have a high sap content and may need extra drying time before use.

groundhogs, and black bears, as well as a summer source of berries for bobwhite quail, wild turkeys, and woodpeckers. Look along old fence lines and crop-field drainage ditches for this walking stick wood. It is a wonderful ornamental yard tree that brings butterflies to your flower and vegetable gardens.

Maple (Acer *sp.*)

Native to Asia, Europe, northern Africa, and North America, there are 128 species of maple, of which 54 are under threat of extinction in their native habitat.

This is a common landscaping tree that grows quickly under many environmental conditions. Maple is a major timber source and also provides sap for maple sugar and Tennessee whiskey. This dense hardwood, with its clean, white coloration, is perfect for use in musical instruments like violins, violas, and cellos. Maple is also a primary pulpwood for paper.

The maple sapling shown here has a long scar where a buck deer used the sapling to rub off the summer velvet from his antlers, adding a bit of interest to an otherwise plain, smooth, pale-gray bark.

Sassafras (Sassafras albidum)

This small deciduous tree, which grows 30 feet (9m) to 50 feet (15m) tall, is native to eastern North America and eastern Asia. The bark of the new branches has a smooth, mid-gray colored texture during its early growth, with the trunk and older branches having a deeply furrowed, red-brown colored bark.

Because of the small size of this tree, it is not a common furniture or woodworking wood. Instead, it is used in creating essential oils for perfume and soaps, as well as acting as the primary ingredient in root beer.

Sassafras is the host plant—the primary food source—for spicebush swallowtail butterflies. It is an excellent winter food for white-tailed deer,

Eastern White Pine
(Pinus strobus)

White pine grows from Newfoundland through the Great Lakes region, Minnesota to Manitoba, and south along the Mississippi Basin to the Appalachian Mountains. It is a fast-growing softwood tree, used for roughing lumber and furniture work, and it is the most common tree for sailing ship masts.

Pine has a clear, white coloring when first cut that darkens to a deep golden orange tone with age. It has wide grain lines with heavy sap areas in the multiple knotholes.

Elm (Ulmus sp.)

Elms are native to the northern hemisphere and are found as both deciduous and semi-deciduous. They grow in a wide diversity of environs, having only one major requirement: good drainage to the soil. It can be difficult to determine which species of elm you might encounter, as this tree easily interbreeds between the 30 or so major species to create micro-species that are native to very small, local regions. In the U.S., the most common species is *Ulmus americana*, a fast-growing landscape tree.

Because of the strength of elm's interlocking grain, it is used in wagon wheels, wagon wheel hubs, chair seats, and coffins.

Rhododendron
(Rhododendron *sp.*)

This small tree species enjoys colder climates and is found from the 80-degree latitude north throughout North America, Europe, Russia, Asia, and some areas of Australia. In its native habitat, rhododendron is found just within the terminal edge of the forest. It prefers some light shade and grows under the taller trees' canopy.

This species has been under cultivation since the mid-1700s and is a common landscaping shrub that does occasionally require pruning. Rhododendron grows multiple small side branches that last for only a few seasons. When the branches die, they leave a raised mound along the side of the main branch, which will add interest to your walking sticks.

Black Cherry (Prunus serotina)

Often considered a weed tree in eastern North America, this species is a major wildlife and songbird food source. It has an extremely rough, broken-looking bark on the main trunk of the tree, but the branches can appear as if they were wrapped in thin sheets of gray-gold paper. Small green and white spotting is common on the very young branch bark. This is a pioneer species, found along old fence lines and hedgerows and in abandoned fields. When possible, choose three- to four-year-old sapling trunks over larger branches to obtain strong, straight staffs.

Black cherry, also called rum cherry or mountain cherry, is used in jams, jellies, and wine, giving a sharper taste than cultivar cherries.

Bamboo *(family Bambusoideae)*

Bamboo is not a tree but a flowering, perennial grass that reproduces from underground rhizomes. There are more than 1,450 species of bamboo, which is native from Southeast Asia through Australia, and it is a common landscaping plant in North America. New shoots begin in the early spring and can grow up to 4 feet (1.2m) in one day. By the end of summer, the average new shoot can reach 30 feet (9m) to 40 feet (12m) in length, depending on the species. Only harvest two-year-old or older growth.

Bamboo is a perfect walking stick wood because it grows in extremely long, straight lengths. You can cut several walking sticks from a single three- to five-year-old cane. Because the sections of bamboo between the branch nodes are hollow, this is a very lightweight but very strong staff material.

Burning Bush (Euonymus alatus)

Burning bush is the common name for a Euonymus cultivar that is used in landscaping. Also called winged euonymus or winged spindle, this bush can easily obtain heights of 10 feet (3m) with a spread of up to 15 feet (4.5m). During fall, the leaves turn a vivid red color, hence the name burning bush. For our use in cane carving, the older stems of the winged euonymus make extremely interesting walking stick shafts. The bark of this euonymus species has protruding ridges that run down the four sides of the branch, thus the name winged euonymus.

Choose main branches that are at least 1" (2.5cm) or wider in growth. Cut the branch as close to the ground as possible to avoid leaving a die-off in the center of the shrub.

Honeysuckle (Lonicera *sp.*)

Honeysuckle is a very common vine found along old fence lines and winding up young saplings. North America enjoys 20 different varieties. This is a major food source for native bees and birds that feast on the berries, and serves as a nesting site for many birds as well. An old honeysuckle vine can become quite thick over the years, producing multiple side shoots.

Although honeysuckle alone is not suitable for cane staffs, it is important to note for any cane carver. These vines twist and twine around young saplings that also inhabit the edges of fields and untended fence lines. As both plants grow, the honeysuckle distorts the sapling into a spiraling, graduated twist that will eventually make an outstanding cane stick.

Preparing a Staff

Here are five different ways you can prepare a staff. Whether you peel the bark, partially peel the bark, or leave the bark on the stick, all preparation methods will eventually be treated the same when it comes time to use either an oil finish or paste wax finish.

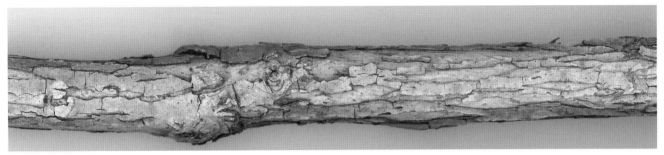

With bark: Leaving the bark on your staff emphasizes the fact that your stick is created from a natural, cut tree. For heavily textured barks, plan for the grip area of the stick to fall on the cane topper instead of the staff itself.

Without bark: It is easy to peel the bark from a freshly cut stick by using a bench knife to loosen a small area of the bark at the top of the stick, then pulling and peeling it away from the wood.

Partially debarked: You can peel the bark off a dried stick in the same manner, but often the bark will come off in much smaller pieces, and some areas may not be completely removed. This can leave the staff with several color tones throughout its surface.

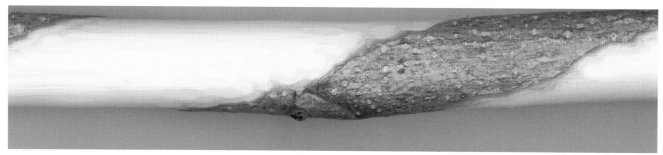

Twist cut bark: While the staff is fresh cut, use a bench knife to peel a spiral strip around the outside of the staff. This creates a spiral of bark twining around the peeled wood section. I often use this type of peeling on smooth-barked woods such as maple or elm.

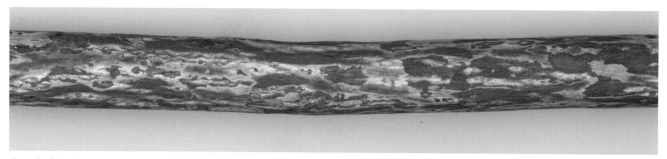

Sanded bark: Rough-textured barks such as black walnut, hickory, and oak can be sanded after the stick is dry. This leaves the bark on the stick while removing the extra-coarse areas of the bark.

Chapter 2: Joinery

Once you have chosen the staff you want to use for your walking stick or cane, you'll have to attach the carved topper to the staff. There are many different methods for doing so, with advantages and disadvantages depending on the ultimate purpose of the piece you are creating. Whether you want to keep it simple with a wooden dowel or precisely measure for using bamboo, you'll find a method to suit your needs in this chapter, plus tips and tricks that will be useful for any cane assembly.

Joinery Basics

Before you begin carving a basswood blank to create a cane topper, you will want to plan how you will join your cane topper to your walking stick. You will need to create the attachment using some form of anchor bolt or dowel and glue. There are several different ways you can accomplish this task, and each has its own advantages and disadvantages. We will look in depth at six options below. But first, three important points will always need to be considered when you are attaching a cane topper to a walking stick: alignment, air space, and glue choice.

Alignment: It is much easier, and more accurate, to mark and drill a hole in your cane topper before you do any carving steps.

Air space: When you drill holes in both the cane topper and the stick, you need to allow a small amount of extra space for the glue and to allow the air inside the hole to escape when you insert the joinery hardware.

Glue choice: Certain glues are more appropriate for certain hardware. If you are using a metal hanger bolt or all thread rod, you will want to glue with two-part epoxy. If you are using a dowel rod or dowel pin, or carving an insert plug on the bottom of your cane topper, you should use wood glue for the joint.

Following are the general steps for attaching any topper to any cane. Depending on the exact hardware/method you choose of the six options in Hardware Joint Options (page 21), these steps will be modified and/or expanded.

General Joinery Instructions

1 Mark the center point on the bottom of the uncarved basswood block. Place the basswood, bottom up, into a vice. Using a dowel jig, drill a rod hole into the block. Rock the drill slightly to widen the drilled hole. This will create a small amount of room between the walls of the hole and the insert to allow air to escape. Repeat to drill a hole into the top of the stick.

2 Work the carving, painting, and finishing steps of the cane topper.

3 Use a bamboo skewer to spread an even layer of glue along the walls of the hole in the stick as well as the walls of the hole in the topper. Proceed with attaching steps, then wipe away any excess glue.

4 Use masking tape or painter's tape to secure the topper and the stick (more detail on page 30). Allow to dry overnight. Add a wrap to hide the joint (more detail on pages 31-39).

Hardware Joint Options

Threaded Rod Joint

There are many ways to attach your cane topper to your stick, but threaded rod gives you the strongest and most durable joint. Threaded rod comes in two styles: solid and hollow.

Solid threaded rod is called all thread rod and is used as a continuous threaded anchor rod in general construction projects. It comes in 12" (30.5cm) to 36" (90.5cm) lengths. For canes and walking sticks, I use ¼" (0.5cm) to ⅜" (1cm) diameter all thread rod, cut into 5" (12.5cm) to 7" (17.5cm) lengths, depending on the height of the topper.

Hollow threaded rod, also called threaded pipe, is a continuous threaded rod with a hollow core. It is used in lamp wiring where the electrical wire can be inserted into the hollow core to hide the cord from view. This style is available in short, precut lengths or in 36" (90.5cm) lengths. It can easily be cut using a hacksaw.

Advantages: Since all thread rod is readily available in 36" (90.5cm) lengths, you can create extra-long anchoring rods for 6" (15cm) or higher cane toppers and for bamboo sticks where you want the anchoring rod to breach more than one node.

Disadvantages: Solid all thread rod does add weight to your walking stick. Although it seems like a minor amount of added weight, it can make the difference between a comfortable stick when in use and one that feels a touch too heavy.

Uses: This particular rod joint is wonderful for canes where the hand rests or holds the cane by the carved topper.

1 Follow step 1 of the general instructions, choosing a drill bit the same size as the width—diameter—of your rod, and one that is at least half the length of the rod.

2 Follow steps 2–4 of the general instructions, using a two-part epoxy as your glue (because you are working with a metal rod).

Double-Ended Wood Screw Threaded Hanger Bolt

A double-ended wood screw hanger bolt can be used to join your cane topper and stick without glue, making the topper detachable. Because this particular hanger bolt is fairly short, the joint is not as strong as a threaded rod or long hardwood dowel joint. Use it for long walking sticks where the grip is below the topper and stick joint.

Advantages: You do not need a drill, drill bit, or dowel-centering jig to use a double-threaded wood screw hanger bolt. Because hanger bolts are usually short in length, less than 1" (2.5cm) on each side of the center, you can choose to use a small or medium-sized round gouge, upended, to create your guide hole in both the topper and stick if you prefer.

Disadvantages: Double-threaded hanger bolts are fairly short in length. You may only have 1½" (3.8cm) to 2" (5cm) of bolt inside each piece of your cane. Under stress, this type of joinery can break through the sides of the cane or topper.

Uses: The double-threaded hanger bolt, in longer lengths, is perfect either for canes where the hand grip is on the topper or for walking sticks where the grip is on the stick. Short-length double-threaded hanger bolts should be used for walking sticks only.

1 Mark the center point of the top of your stick and the bottom of your topper with a pencil.

2 Choose a drill bit the same size or one size smaller than the width of your hanger bolt. Drill a hole into both the topper and the stick, slightly longer than half the length of the bolt—half of the bolt will be going into the topper and half into the stick. Alternatively, you can create the holes with a round gouge. Choose a round gouge that is the same size or slightly larger than the width of your hanger bolt. Hold the gouge vertical to the wood and roll the cutting edge into the wood. After you have cut a circular line into the wood, use the gouge to remove the wood inside the circle. Repeat until you have cut the hole slightly deeper than the length of the threaded side that will be inserted into the wood.

3 Using pliers, grip the hanger bolt in the top section of wood screw threads. Screw the bottom portion of the bolt into the stick until only the top threaded area is above the stick.

4 Grip the bolt as closely as possible to the stick with pliers. Holding the bolt in place, hand screw the topper onto the hanger bolt. When the topper touches the pliers, remove the pliers and continue screwing the topper onto the stick until the two touch.

5 If you choose to add glue to this joint, use two-part epoxy.

Machine-Threaded Hanger Bolt with Nut

This hanger bolt has one side machine-threaded to receive a nut and the other side threaded as a wood screw to bite into the wood. Because you are working with a metal rod, use two-part epoxy as your glue.

Advantages: This type of joint does have the great advantage that the cane topper can be removed from the walking stick without damaging either portion. Since only the nut of the hanger bolt is glued into the topper, you can exchange toppers for a favorite stick or preserve your cane topper carving if the stick becomes damaged.

Disadvantages: This hanger bolt hardware uses only ½" (1.5cm) of bolt inside the cane topper and 1½" (3.8cm) of bolt inside the cane stick. Because the bolt is short, this particular joinery is not very strong and should be used only on tall walking sticks where the hand grip is below the cane topper portion of the stick.

Uses: I suggest this particular joinery for decorative canes or extra-long walking sticks. It does not have the strength to be used in a cane where the grip is on the topper.

1 Drill a hole into both the cane topper and the cane stick the size of the hanger bolt. Thread the nut onto the machine screw. Place the machine screw end into the cane topper and mark where the outside edge of the nut falls on the bottom of the topper. With a bench knife and chisels, cut the bottom of the topper to fully receive the nut.

2 Remove the nut from the machine side of the hanger bolt. Use quick-set epoxy to set the nut into the bottom of the cane topper. Avoid getting any epoxy into the nut threads. Allow the epoxy to dry completely.

3 Using a bamboo skewer, apply a thin layer of epoxy glue to the joinery hole in the cane stick. Insert the wood screw section of the hanger bolt into the cane stick until only the machine-threaded area shows above the stick. Allow the epoxy to dry completely.

4 To make the insertion of the wood screw section of the bolt easier, screw the nut onto the machine-threaded section. Grip the nut in pliers and use the pliers to screw the wood screw section into place. Once the bolt is set, remove the nut immediately and allow the epoxy to dry.

5 The cane topper can be screwed onto the cane stick by threading the machine-threaded area of the hanger into the glued nut in the topper.

Long Hardwood Dowel Rods

Hardwood dowels are readily available at both craft stores and your local hardware store. They come in 36" (90.5cm) lengths and vary in diameter. I prefer, whenever possible, to use a ⅜" (1cm) diameter dowel. Dowels can be cut in any length, so they are perfect for use with any sized cane topper.

Advantages: Hardwood dowels are extremely strong, yet allow for a small amount of give under stress. This means that your joinery will hold up under hard use without breaking. Dowel rods are easy to cut with a bench knife, so no woodworking tools are needed beyond your normal carving kit tools.

Disadvantages: Wood-glued hardwood dowels create a permanent joint. If you want to retrieve your topper at a later date, you will need to use a saw to remove the topper from the stick and then drill out the dowel from the topper.

Uses: A long hardwood dowel joint can be used for any walking stick or cane.

1 Follow step 1 of the general instructions, making sure the drilled holes are about ¹⁄₁₆" (0.2cm) larger than your dowel.

2 Follow steps 2–4 of the general instructions, using wood glue. The water in the wood glue will penetrate the dowel, causing it to swell slightly and create a tighter joint between the dowel and the stick.

Short Fluted Dowel Pins

Fluted dowel pins can be purchased at your local hardware store and come in a variety of diameters and lengths. Usually they are sold in packets of twelve.

Dowel pins are created by compressing the wood into the dowel pin shape. When the pin is saturated with wood glue, it swells, forcing an extremely tight joint between the sides of the pin and the stick. The fluted ribs and the rounded ends of a dowel pin allow air to escape from the joinery holes and create more surface space for gluing.

Advantages: Dowel pins are extremely easy to use in your walking sticks and canes. Most dowel pins are short enough that you can cut the joinery hole using a round gouge. Even though dowel pins are short in length, they create a very durable, strong joint, even under stress.

Disadvantages: Most fluted dowel pins come in very short lengths of 3" (7.5cm) or less. They will not create a strong joint for very tall cane toppers that are 6" (15cm) tall or taller. For extra-tall toppers, create your own fluted dowel pins by cutting several V-troughs in a hardwood dowel using

your V-gouge or U-gouge. By cutting your own fluting, you have both the advantages of the hardwood dowel and the air passages and added surface area of a fluted dowel.

Uses: Short fluted dowels are excellent for smaller toppers on long walking sticks. Handmade hardwood fluted dowels can be used on any walking stick or cane.

1 Follow the same instructions as used for the Long Hardwood Dowel Rods method.

Topper Plug and Anchor Bolt

The more surface area you have for gluing, the stronger your joint will be. One way to increase surface area is to cut the bottom 1" (2.5cm) or more of your cane topper into a plug that can be inserted into a carved hole in the top of the stick. (See more detail on creating this type of joint on page 27.)

Advantages: Cutting a plug at the bottom of your topper lets you bring portions of the topper down and over the stick area. A beard and mustache on the topper, for example, can extend beyond the plug area so that they flow into the stick. A plug joint is also extremely strong.

Disadvantages: Cutting a plug joint does add planning and cutting time to the creation of your cane, so allow a couple of extra hours for whittling and fitting this joint.

Uses: A plug joint is particularly good for joinery with a bamboo stick. The plug can be cut to exactly fit the open center of the bamboo and cut to the length needed to touch the closing of the bamboo at the top node. The bamboo sample shown on page 28 uses a hardwood dowel as the anchor for a plug joint.

1 When planning your plug, try to allow ¼" (0.5cm) of wood along the outer edge of the stick hole. The longer the plug is, the stronger the joint.

2 Begin by marking the center point in both the cane topper and the staff with a pencil. Use a drill, dowel-set jig, and a drill bit the same size or slightly larger than your hanger bolt to create a hole in each piece to receive the joinery hardware.

3 On the bottom of your cane topper blank, mark a pencil line that shows where the staff will lie against the topper. Mark a second pencil line ¼" (0.5cm) in from the first line to note how wide your plug area will be. The area or space between these two circular lines will be cut, using your bench knife and round gouges, to a depth of at least ½" (1.5cm) or more. Any area outside the outer circular line on your cane topper can be used to create and carve details on your topper that will fall over the staff area. As an example, the outer area of the topper can become a portion of a wood spirit's beard that falls over the cane staff.

4 Repeat step 2 on the top surface of the staff. The area inside the inner circular pencil line will be cut to receive the cane topper plug, using your bench knife and round gouges to a matching depth to the cane topper plug.

5 After the plug has been carved into the topper and the plug hole cut into the stick, you can use a double-threaded wood screw hanger bolt or a machine-threaded hanger bolt and nut as a central anchor rod.

Sample Topper Plug Joint

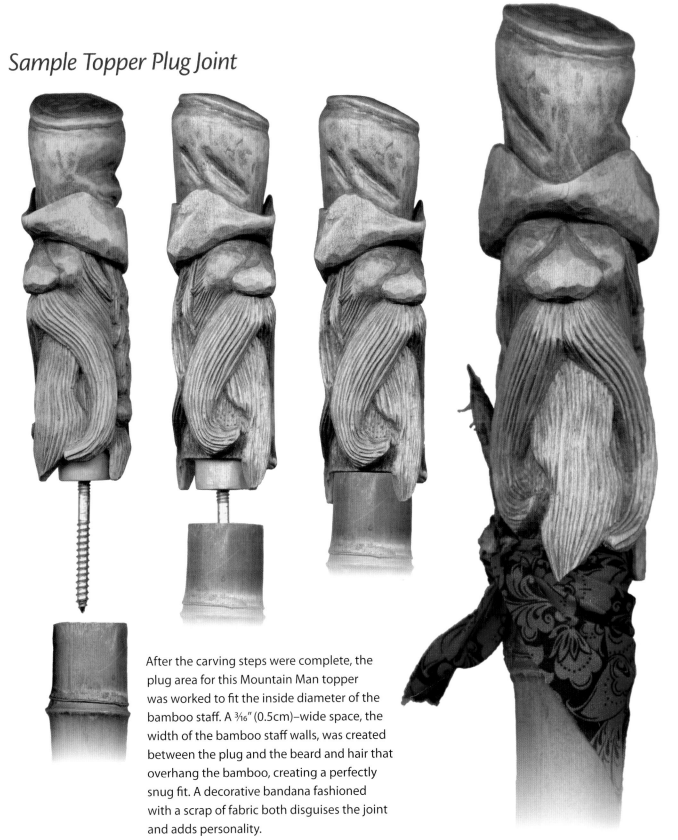

After the carving steps were complete, the plug area for this Mountain Man topper was worked to fit the inside diameter of the bamboo staff. A ³⁄₁₆" (0.5cm)–wide space, the width of the bamboo staff walls, was created between the plug and the beard and hair that overhang the bamboo, creating a perfectly snug fit. A decorative bandana fashioned with a scrap of fabric both disguises the joint and adds personality.

Working with Bamboo

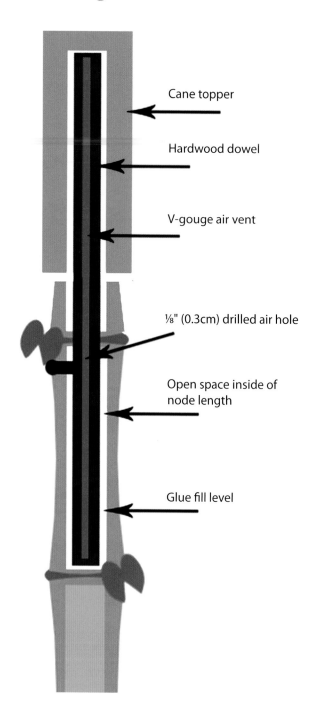

Cane topper

Hardwood dowel

V-gouge air vent

⅛" (0.3cm) drilled air hole

Open space inside of node length

Glue fill level

Bamboo is lightweight, easy to cut, and available in extra-long lengths, making it perfect for walking sticks. Because bamboo is hollow between the branch nodes, special attention is needed when attaching a carved cane topper. Here is a method to make your cane construction easy and secure when using bamboo.

1 Be careful when working with bamboo that you have harvested. Over the drying time, it can develop several types of fungus and black mold or become infested with insects. If the cane is completely black or completely white with mold, dispose of it. A small amount of discoloration is normal.

2 Wash the cane with a dishwashing detergent solution, rinse, and dry with a cloth. For a moderately discolored cane, lightly scrub with a steel wool pad.

3 Measure ½" (1.5cm) above the largest node—joint space— of the cane and cut along that line to trim the excess cane. Hold the cane upside down on a piece of coarse sandpaper and sand the cut line smooth. This end is where the cane topper will go.

4 Drill a ¼" (0.5cm)–wide hole into this top node space.

5 Drill a ¼" (0.5cm)–wide hole into the bottom of the wood cane topper. Drill as deeply as your drill bit will allow. I rock my drill bit after I have made the first cuts to widen the hole slightly. This allows space inside the cane topper for both the hardwood dowel and the glue.

6 The spaces between the bamboo nodes are hollow air spaces. To allow the air to escape as you add the glue and the hardwood dowel, drill a small ⅛" (0.3cm) hole into the side of the bamboo cane just under the first side branch node.

7 Dry-test your dowel in the cane topper, marking a pencil line on the dowel at the base of the topper. Remove the dowel and cut two V-gouge lines on either side of the dowel. These V-gouge lines, just like the drilled side hole in the bamboo, will allow air and excess glue to escape when the dowel is set.

8 Add glue inside the dowel hole in the topper. I use a bamboo kitchen skewer for this job. For this cane, I chose wood glue, but you may also use epoxy or another kind of glue; follow the manufacturer's instructions. Insert the dowel into the cane topper, and then wipe away any excess glue at the base with a damp cloth.

9 The node space for this example bamboo stick is about 12" (30.5cm) long. If you just add glue at the top node, the remainder of the dowel will be suspended unattached in that air space. To secure the bottom section of the cane dowel, fill the node space with enough glue to cover at least the lower 1" (2.5cm) of the dowel. When the glue dries, the bottom point of the dowel will be secure.

10 Using masking tape or painter's tape, clamp the cane topper tightly to the bamboo stick (see page 30). Allow the glue to dry thoroughly, for at least 24 hours.

11 After the glue is set, remove the tape clamp. Your walking stick is ready to paint and finish.

Easy Tape Clamp

Masking tape, fiber packing tape, and painter's tape can be used as gluing clamps to secure a cane topper to a stick once the joint has been created. Follow this simple procedure to create a tape "clamp" to make sure your finished joint is always snug and secure.

1 After the dowel or anchor bolt has been inserted and the glue applied, cut several extra-long lengths of tape. Attach the top edge of each of the tape strips above the glue joint on the topper. Wrap one piece of tape around these top edges to cover and secure them.

2 Cut a long piece of tape and wrap it horizontally once around the stick, below the glue joint. Working one vertical strip at a time, pull the vertical strip down along the side of the cane and secure it by wrapping the lower horizontal strip over it. Repeat for each vertical strip.

3 Allow the cane to dry overnight, then remove the tape.

Chapter 3: Joint Covers

When you carve a cane or walking stick, you give each area of the work special attention, keeping in mind the final owner. You have carefully picked a theme or topic to carve, the type of wood, and even the length of the staff for its final use. So it's no time to forget about the joints and grips! You can cover up joints as well as add comfortable hand grips by wrapping with leather or cord in a variety of ways, all of which you'll learn in this chapter.

Wrapping Basics

Joint wraps serve three important purposes for cane topper walking sticks: strength, grip, and decoration.

A glued dowel joint is extremely strong, but by adding a tight wrapping over that joint area, you can add more strength. The wrap protects the glue line from accumulated dirt, wear, and tear that, over time, can loosen the area.

Often, a walking stick will have a finishing coat of spray sealer, brush-on polyurethane, or paste wax. All three brighten the natural look of the wood as well as protect the coloring of the topper from hand dirt and UV light. But all three of these types of sealers are slick to the touch, which means that your hand will slide easily across the stick's surface. Adding a wrapping adds texture to the hand area of the stick to give the user better gripping power.

As carvers, we work our favorite themes as we carve and create any walking stick. Often, the end user also wants to add their own touches to give that stick a more personal flavor. The end strings of a wrapping (as shown in Lanyard Wrapping, page 36) can be used to add feathers, beads, shells, cut walnut hulls, and even little totem carvings—whatever the user desires.

Leather has long been traditional as the wrapping material for sticks. It is available in a wide range of colors through leather crafting companies, jewelry supply stores, and large craft outlets, in small lengths from 1 to 5 yards (1 to 5m) up to large spools of 50 yards (50m). It can be sold as leather round cord, leather lacing, latigo lacing, and suede lacing.

Other **natural fibers** include bailing twine, hemp cord, waxed sinew, craft twine, and polished twine. Small-diameter twines can be purchased in a wide color range, but larger cording is sold predominately in natural beige to brown tones.

Rattail cord, rubber beading cord, faux leather cord, and paracord are **synthetic fibers** that perform well with long-term use.

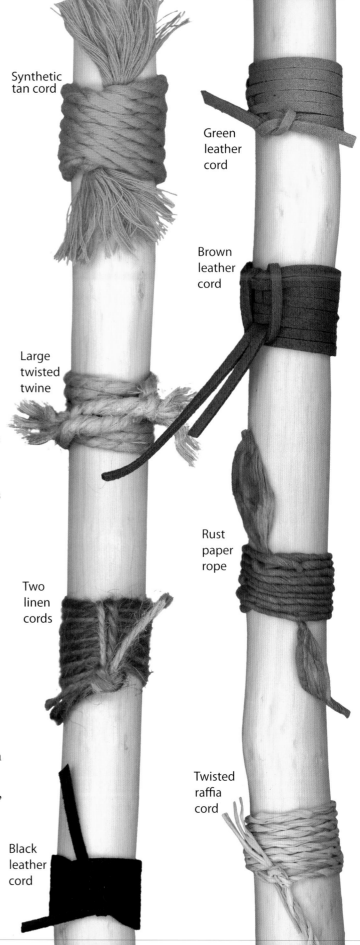

Synthetic tan cord

Green leather cord

Brown leather cord

Large twisted twine

Rust paper rope

Two linen cords

Twisted raffia cord

Black leather cord

Simple Leather Grip Wrapping

When you are carving a hiking stick, staff, or walking stick, a leather string grip is a nice finishing touch to your work. The leather wrap provides extra strength in the grip when the staff is in use. The leather string wrap is put on after all other work is complete. It should be positioned where the most comfortable hand grip is along the length of the staff and extend several inches in either direction of the width of the hand. You will need several yards of leather string, obtainable from any leather craft supplier or most local craft stores.

1 Soak the leather string in warm water for about ten minutes to get it completely soaked. Then pat on a clean towel to remove the excess water.

2 Starting at the top of the walking stick, hold the leather string against the staff. Allow 3" (7.5cm) or 4" (10cm) of string to extend away from the cane at point A.

3 Pull the leather down the staff to pass the wrap area by several inches. Fold the leather back on itself up to point A. This creates a loop at the bottom of the wrap area.

4 Cross the leather string over the original end at point A and begin wrapping it around the staff. The crossover anchors the end during wrapping.

5 When you reach the end of the wrap area, insert the second end of the leather string through the loop you created in step 3.

6 Holding onto the end of the string at point B, pull on the excess string at point A. The top end of the string will pull the bottom end of the string underneath the wrapped string area. This anchors and hides the joining area of the wrap.

7 Allow the wrap to dry completely, overnight. As it dries, it will shrink and grasp firmly to the staff.

8 Once the leather string is completely dry, you can cut the end strings where they touch the wrap. You now have a permanent and strong leather string wrap with no knots or ties showing.

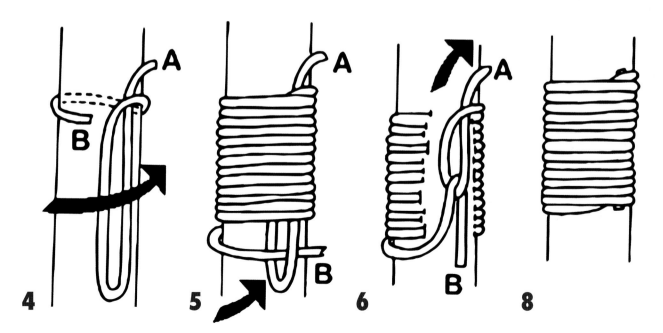

Cord Wrapping

This super simple cord wrap is quick and easy, and can also serve as an emergency supply of rope if you're in need out in the woods!

1 Using ¼" (0.5cm)–thick craft twine, untwist the first 2" (5cm) to avoid a thick area in the top wrapping. Lay that opened end of the twine on a diagonal, facing downward, where you want the top edge of the wrap on your stick.

3 Since this staff is bamboo, the wrapping will have a gap where it jumps under the node branch cuts.

2 Hold the open end and begin rolling the stick to create three to five nice, tight coils, working each coil over the untwisted end. Cut any excess untwisted end with a bench knife.

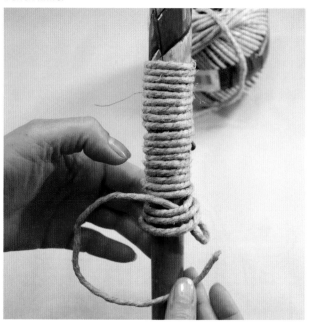

4 Continue wrapping for whatever length of wrap you desire. A 3" (7.5cm) wrap will strengthen the glue joint; a 5" (12.5cm) wrap is large enough to become a full hand grip for a medium-sized hand; a 7" (17.5cm) wrap suits a larger hand. When you reach your desired length, cut the twine about 12" (30.5cm) from the last coil. Loosen the bottom three coils of the wrap and thread the end of the twine under these coils.

5 Holding the end of the twine, re-tighten the three bottom coils.

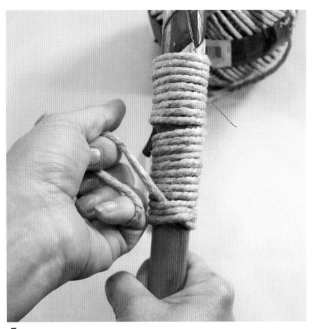

6 Give the cord a strong pull to pull the end of the twine under the last three coils.

7 Use a bench knife to cut the excess end twine by slicing between the coils.

8 This wrap uses about 2 yards (2m) of twine and is not glued to the stick. If you ever need some quick rope on a hike, you can tease one end out of the wrap and use that rope!

Lanyard Wrapping

This lanyard wrap will allow you or the user of the stick to add personalized embellishments with ease.

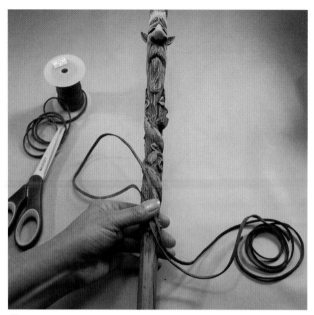

1 Cut 2 yards (2m) of ¼" (0.5cm) suede leather cording. This piece will become the lanyard to your wrap. Fold the cord in half and position a 7" (17.5cm) loop 1" (2.5cm) above the glue joint.

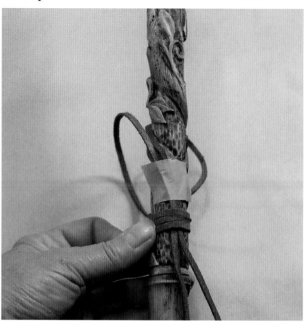

2 Place a small piece of masking tape over the base of the loop to hold it in place. Lay the end of the wrapping suede over the lanyard on a diagonal, facing the bottom of the stick. Coil the wrapping suede three times around the stick, tightly covering the lanyard cords.

3 Using a bench knife, cut the excess diagonal end cord. Bring the wrapping cord to the lanyard ends, lift the lanyard cords, and coil the wrapping leather under the lanyard ends. Wrap a second coil, but this time wrap it over the lanyard ends.

4 Continue wrapping in this under/over pattern for 5" (12.5cm). Adjust the spacing and tension of the coils as you work. End the wrapping pattern with an over coil.

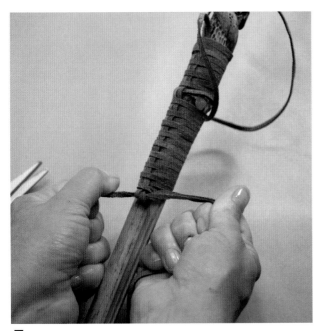

5 Tie the wrapping cord to the lanyard cords in a square knot. Pull tightly to set the knot.

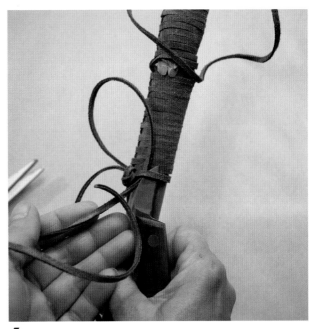

6 Use a bench knife or scissors to lift the last coil in the wrap. Thread all three cords over the knot, then through the lifted coil to set them in a downward position. Pull the cords tightly to set them in place.

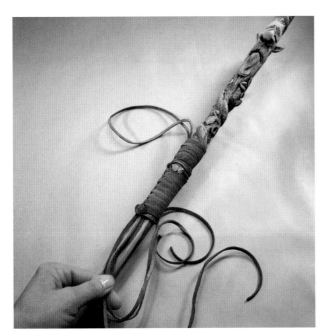

7 Cut all three cords to approximately 18" (45.5cm) long. The long length provides plenty of room to add accents such as beads, shells, or trinkets.

More Joint Ideas

Here are three more joint techniques that you can use to finish your cane topper sticks.

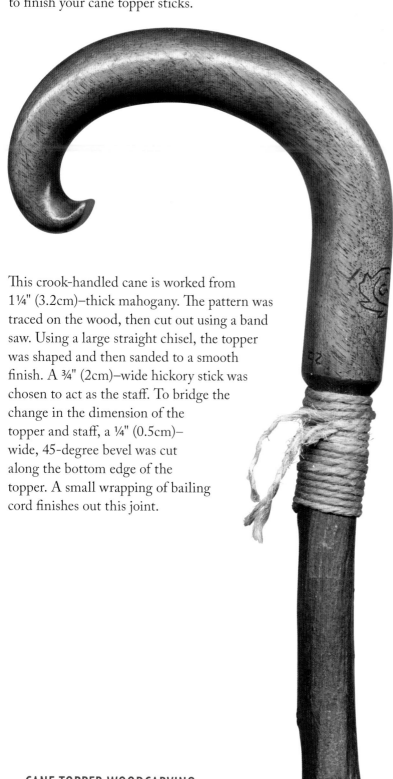

This crook-handled cane is worked from 1¼" (3.2cm)–thick mahogany. The pattern was traced on the wood, then cut out using a band saw. Using a large straight chisel, the topper was shaped and then sanded to a smooth finish. A ¾" (2cm)–wide hickory stick was chosen to act as the staff. To bridge the change in the dimension of the topper and staff, a ¼" (0.5cm)–wide, 45-degree bevel was cut along the bottom edge of the topper. A small wrapping of bailing cord finishes out this joint.

This cane topper stick does not try to hide or disguise the joint. Instead, a space was used between the two main parts of the cane as an accent area. The topper was cut on a band saw from 1¼" (3.2cm)–wide mahogany, shaped with a chisel, and then sanded. The staff of the stick was worked from a 1¼" x 1¼" x 36" (3.2 x 3.2 x 90.5cm) length of ash. To create the spacer, a 1¼" x 1¼" x ½" (3.2 x 3.2 x 1.5cm) piece of black walnut was cut. All three areas were drilled to receive the joint rod or dowel. During the gluing steps, the black walnut spacer was inserted between the topper and staff. After the glue had set, the joint area, including the bottom of the cane topper, the spacer, and the staff, was chiseled and sanded to give a smooth transition from the topper to the staff.

This antler stick does not hide or disguise the joint area either. The exposed joint emphasizes that this stick is created using two different materials—deer antler and hickory wood. The hand grip area was created using a 4" x 5" (10 x 12.5cm) piece of ⅛" (0.3cm)–thick leather. Threading holes, ¹⁄₁₆" (0.2cm) in diameter, were punched along the two long sides with ¼" (0.5cm) of spacing between each hole. The leather was soaked for ten minutes in water, and then blotted on a clean towel to remove the excess water. Using waxed sinew, the grip was laced into position 1½" (3.8cm) from the cane joint. As the lacing was worked, it was pulled firmly but not overtightened, just enough to bring the two sides of the leather into contact. As the leather dried, it shrank just enough to take on the contour and shape of the stick.

Chapter 4: Extras

Canes and walking sticks can be customized in a variety of ways beyond the essential features of staff, topper, and grip. In this chapter, you'll find ideas for useful tool bags, charming pipes, wood and wire accessories, tips for the bases of your canes, and how to personalize a grip. With any or all of these extra features, each of your finished pieces will shine as unique works of art.

"What If" Bags

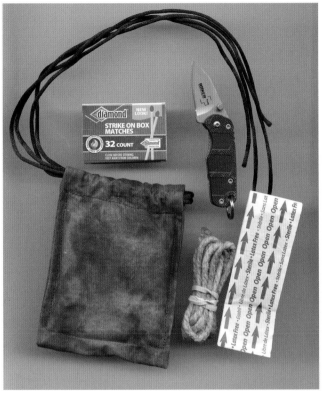

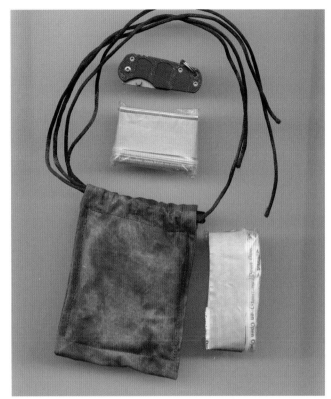

Give your walking sticks that little extra touch by adding a quick and easy "What If" bag. My personal bag (above) is filled with a few small items that I might need along the hiking trail: bandages, cord, matches, and a folding pocketknife. You can also use it as a small collecting bag, to hold your cell phone or car keys, or to just keep a snack close at hand.

The bag shown left is created using two 5 ½" x 12" (14 x 30.5cm) pieces of cotton quilting fabric with rattail cord as a drawstring. The bag has a folded pocket along the bottom edge for a second drawstring to keep the bag from swinging as the walking stick moves. You can buy premade cotton canvas and cotton muslin bags in a variety of sizes at your local craft store.

The bag shown right is 4" x 6" (10 x 15cm) and also uses rattail cord as a drawstring tie. The bag holds a plastic bag of bandages and 2 yards (2m) of heavy cotton cord held together with two large rubber bands. A second plastic bag is wrapped around a box of strike-anywhere matches. A small, sharpened pocketknife is included. You may also wish to add a little emergency money in the form of a folded $10 bill inside one of the plastic bags. A large safety pin closes the top of the bag.

If you sell your walking sticks and canes at arts and crafts shows, adding a "What If" bag to your creations will make your work stand out from the competition. Create a small display of items your customer can pack in their walking stick bags or include a printed suggestion list with the sale of each cane.

Suggested Materials for a "What If" Bag

- 4" (10cm) to 5" (12.5cm)–wide cotton fabric bag
- 2 yards (2m) of 2mm rattail cord or paracord for the drawstring
- 2 yards (2m) of ¼" (0.5cm) cotton twine
- 2 large rubber bands
- 4 adhesive bandages
- 1 package of strike-anywhere wooden matches
- 1 small pocketknife
- Two 3" x 4" (7.5 x 10cm) zip-top plastic bags
- Two 1" x 4" (2.5 x 10cm) strips of masking tape
- 1 large safety pin

"What If" bags can be both functional and decorative.

Pipes

Consider adding a charming pipe to the character on your cane topper to give an extra boost of personality. Here's how I ended up adding one to this Mountain Man.

Since I have lots of walking sticks, I decided to make this Mountain Man into a talking stick (or speaker's staff) with a short, 16" (40.5cm) staff. After finishing the carving, which is worked on a 1½" x 1½" x 6" (3.8 x 3.8 x 15cm) basswood block, I drilled the ⅜" (1cm) mounting holes for the hardwood joining dowel. Then I dry-checked the fit, testing to be sure that the dowel fit tight and square to both the staff and the carving. My beloved hubby, Michael, was watching me work, and commented, "What that little old man needs is a long cherry wood pipe!" I knew instantly he was absolutely right, so I headed off into our woods to find a cherry branch the right size for my carving. I cut the branch as shown in the photo above right, and then cut a shallow hole in the top of the pipe area for the bowl.

With a 3/16" (0.5cm) drill bit, I created a hole in the bottom side of the pipe where it would touch the talking stick and a hole in the stick at the same place. A 1" (2.5cm) piece of 3/16" (0.5cm) dowel could then be set into the pipe bottom to anchor and secure it to the staff.

To strengthen the pipe bit in the mouth, I used a small round gouge to create a hole in the underside of the mustache so that about ½" (1.5cm) of cherry wood stem could be set into the carving.

With wood glue, I set the hardwood dowel for the cane topper and the talking stick staff. Next, using 1 yard (1m) of ⅛" (0.3cm) rawhide leather cord, I wrapped the joint between the carving and the staff.

The completed cane now has two joining dowels: one to secure the carving to the talking stick staff, and one to join the bottom of the pipe to the staff. The hole inside the mustache area is large enough to allow my pipe to shift and shrink slightly as it dries. The leather rawhide disguises the joint line between the carving and the stick.

Because my cherry wood pipe is fresh-cut wood, it is only dry-set into place. In a couple of months, after the cherry dries well, I will glue it into its final position.

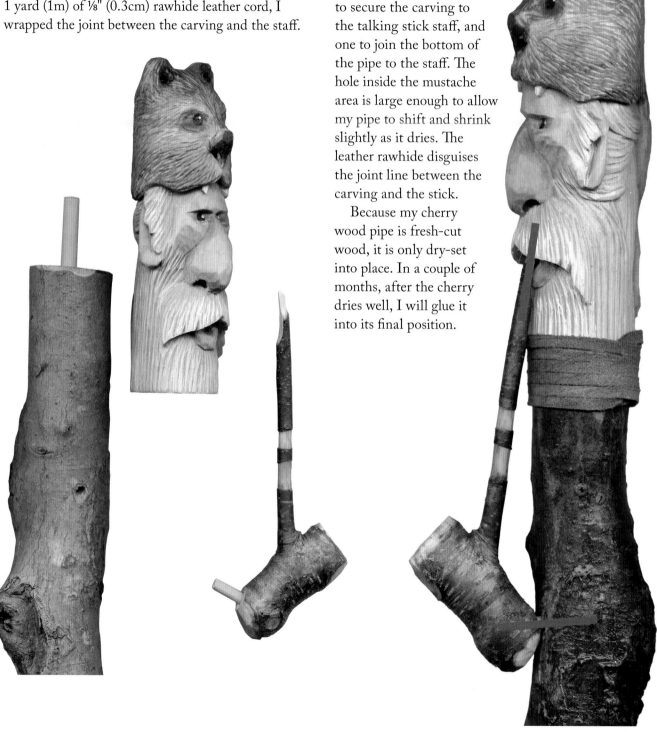

Additional Wood

We often hear the phrase "coloring outside the lines." This idea is very relevant for walking stick carvers. Adding carved elements to the main carving block breaks the finished design free from the confines of the tall, narrow rectangle shape that is usually the basis of a cane topper carving.

To attach additional wood to your carvings, create a miniature dowel rod using a round toothpick. Cut a small section from the center of the toothpick, from ¼" (0.5cm) to ½" (1.5cm) long, depending on the size of the addition. Drill a hole into both the main wood and the addition to accept the miniature dowel. Add glue to both ends of the dowel and attach the addition to the main carving.

The Wood Elf cane topper here shows a simple example of an added carved element. The original practice stick for this piece was a 1" x 1" x 12" (2.5 x 2.5 x 30.5cm) basswood block. To exaggerate the wood elf's nose, a small block— 1" x 1" x 2" (2.5 x 2.5 x 5cm)—was carved into the nose shape. The back side of the nose was sanded to a smooth, flat finish.

Next, using wood glue, the nose was attached to the practice stick and allowed to dry overnight to ensure a firm, solid set. After the glue was dry, the carving block was ready for the remaining carving steps.

Gluing the additional element to the practice block before any of the carving work begins allows you to work with the flat back of the nose and the flat surface of the carving block—no sizing, shaping, or fitting is necessary.

Wire Elements

Don't be afraid to think past just wood. Wire is cheap and easily manipulated to create a variety of accents. Pick up jewelry wire in thick and thin gauges at any jewelry supply or craft store.

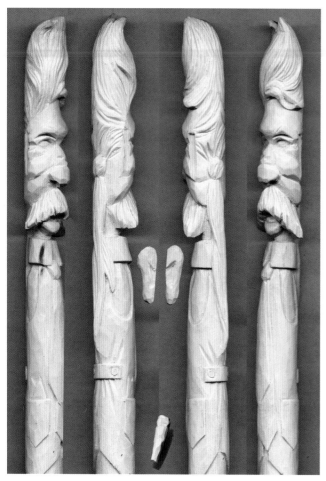

To give this Mark Twain walking stick a set of copper wire glasses, I needed to first give him ears on which to rest those glasses. After the carving of the face itself was completed, I created those ears from a ⅛" x ½" x 1" (0.3 x 1.5 x 2.5cm) basswood board.

In the side of the carved topper, in the ear position, I cut a receiving trough using my smallest chisel. I applied glue to the straight, uncarved side of each ear and set the ears in place. A small stripe of masking tape kept the ears clamped until the glue set.

Actually making the wire glasses wasn't difficult at all. Here's how I did it:

1 Straighten a 12" (30.5cm) length of 18-gauge copper wire using nylon-grip straight pliers. Grip the middle point of the wire in round-nosed pliers and roll the wire over one side of the pliers to create a small, full circle. Reposition the round-nosed pliers to hold the wire adjacent to the small circle you just made, and create a second small circle, turning the wire in the opposite direction from the first.

2 Use the tip of the round-nosed pliers to bend the copper wire at the outer edges of each circle to a 90-degree angle, creating the side pieces of the glasses. Set the wire glasses on the cane topper face to determine where you need to make the ear curves. Grip the wire in the round-nosed pliers and make a half-circle for each ear piece. Clip the excess wire from the ear piece curves using flush wire cutters.

3 After your carving is complete and you have worked any painting steps, set the glasses in place on the face with a drop of superglue at the top of each ear curve arm.

Finally, the receiving trough for Mr. Twain's cigar was created with a small round gouge, upended to cut a perfect circle in the mouth.

Cane Tips

Cane tips are available at most large hardware stores and add a little bit of extra security to the base of your stick. They are available in a variety of diameters and can accept a small screw through the center of the tip that will hold the tip permanently to the staff.

Personalized Grips

As a woodcarver, you can give your canes something truly special by carving the sides of the cane topper to specifically fit the hand of the user.

In the rough-out stage of this wood spirit topper, I decided that it would become one of my personal canes. To make the central grip area of the topper exactly fit my hand and grip, I dipped my hand in water, then picked up the topper as I would a cane. My wet fingerprints showed me exactly where I needed to cut the dips and indents to accept each finger of my grip. I marked the wet areas with a pencil, then used a large round gouge to make those subtle but present grip indents.

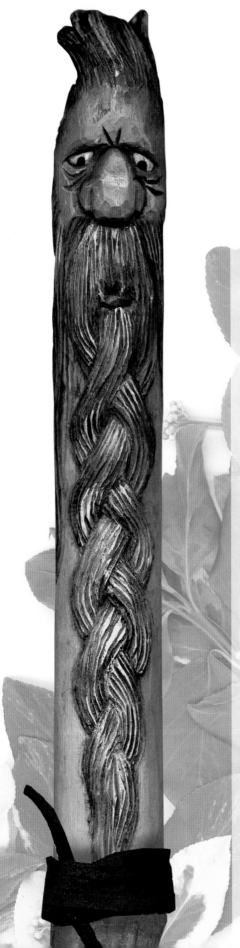

Chapter 5: Topper Carving Basics

While this book isn't meant for total novice carvers, it's still important to review the basic good practices of carving, the knives you'll want to use while working through the projects in this book, safety, some basic useful cuts, and other carving details that are sometimes overlooked. Even if you have a lot of experience carving, read through this chapter as a refresher and to pick up some tips you might not have encountered. If you're a beginner, study this chapter carefully and practice working with the knives and wood before tackling any projects.

Getting Started

Many of the general supplies that you will need for cane topper carving are common household tools or tools using in other crafts such as painting or woodworking. Below is a list of general supplies you may want to have on hand to make your carving an easy and pleasant experience. You may not need all of the below all the time, but, depending on the exact project you are working, you will need many of them.

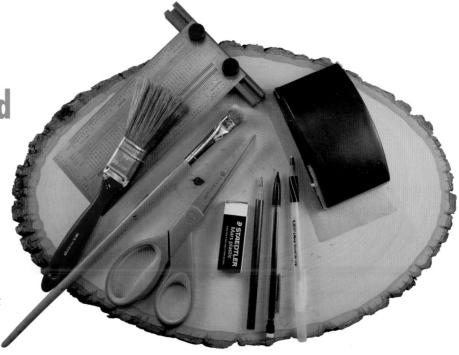

Many cane topper carving supplies are common household tools. Shown here from left to right are a T-square ruler, a large dusting brush, a small ox-hair dusting brush, scissors, a white artist's eraser, assorted pens and pencils, and a sanding block with fine 220-grit sandpaper.

Basswood blocks:

- For cane toppers: 1" x 1" x 3" (2.5 x 2.5 x 7.5cm) through 2" x 2" x 12" (5 x 5 x 30.5cm)
- For hardwood dowels or harvested sticks: 1" (2.5cm) or 1½" (3.8cm) diameter x your desired height

Carving knives:

- Bench knife or large chip carving knife
- V-gouge
- Small round gouge

Sharpening tools:

- Coarse sharpening stone
- Fine sharpening stone
- Leather strop
- Honing rouge or stropping compound
- Emery cloth in assorted grits

Safety tools:

- Kevlar carving gloves
- Thumb protector
- Heavyweight terry cloth towel

Miscellaneous household items:

- Graphite paper
- 220- and 320-grit sandpaper
- Brown paper bag
- Scissors
- Transparent tape
- Pencil and/or pen for tracing and drawing
- Dusting brush
- Acrylic paints in assorted colors
- Acrylic or polyurethane spray sealer

Basswood Carving Blocks

While you can carve with any favorite carving wood, I strongly recommend precut basswood carving blocks for your first cane toppers. Basswood, while classified as a hardwood species, is a soft, easy-to-cut wood. It has long, fine, tightly packed grain that seldom shows a knothole or major imperfection. It accepts very fine V-gouge strokes and can be sanded cleanly and crisply with 220- to 320-grit sandpaper. Its white coloring makes it perfect for painting with either acrylic craft paints or oil stains. Working with a precut size means that you as a hobbyist do not need to cut or plane a larger block down to your desired size. The patterns in this book were all worked from precut basswood blocks in readily available sizes. Other excellent carving woods for cane toppers include butternut, sugar pine, soft maple, and yellow cedar.

Sizing Cane Toppers

You can size the diameter of your cane toppers in two different ways. Just remember that while walking and hiking sticks can be worked in a diameter of up to 2" (5cm), the wider or thicker the topper and staff are, the heavier your stick will be to carry.

One way to size a cane topper is to make it to fit a specific carving blank that you have on hand. For example, if you have a basswood practice block that measures 1" x 1" x 12" (2.5 x 2.5 x 30.5cm), you can size your pattern to be 1" (2.5cm) wide or less. The staff that you will use will also need to be 1" (2.5cm) in diameter or less to easily transition the topper into the staff.

Alternatively, if you have a specific size of hardwood dowel or harvested sapling to use as a staff, then the diameter of that staff will determine the width of the pattern and carving block that you should use.

Measuring the Center Point for the Grip

Canes, which are often held or gripped on the top of the topper, are measured from the floor to the front top of the hipbone for the center point of the grip area.

Walking sticks, on the other hand, are measured to the height of your arm, bent level to the floor for the center point of the grip. Hiking sticks and working sticks (such as shepherd's crooks and orchard sticks) can be cut at shoulder height or taller. The grip is measured with the arm bent upward in a natural position (about 20 degrees above level) for the grip. These three stick styles can have the grip fall on either the cane topper or on a section of the staff.

Knives

Bench Knives and Chip Carving Knives

Bench knives are the primary cutting tool for cane carving. Their straight-edged blades vary in length from ¾" (2cm) to 2" (5cm) long. A complete cane topper can be done using just a bench knife or chip carving knife. Shown in the photo from top to bottom are: a small chip carving knife; a large chip carving knife; a detail knife; a short-blade bench knife; and a long-blade bench knife.

Round Gouges

Round gouges are divided into three categories, which are defined by the arc of the curved cutting edge: wide sweep gouges, round gouges, and U-gouges. With a tight half-circle arc to their cutting edge, the U-gouge or veining tool cuts very fine detail lines and reaches into deep, tight spaces. Round gouges have a medium arc, approximately one-quarter-circle turn, making them perfect for rough-out background work. Wide sweep gouges, also called spoon or fishtail gouges, have a long, low-angled arc. They are excellent for background work and for shaping convex curves.

The tools shown in the photo from left to right are: a small round gouge; a skew chisel (see Chisels, below); a V-gouge (see V-Gouges, below); a bent-shaft straight chisel (see Chisels, below); a large round gouge; and a U-gouge (also called a veining tool). This collection of tools represents a basic beginner's set of carving tools.

Chisels

Straight chisels, skew chisels, and bull nose chisels all feature a straight-line cutting edge. The top side of the tool's edge is beveled to cut deeply along the sides of your elements during the rounding-over process.

The back side of the chisel is flat or even with the tool's shaft. Used as the cutting edge, the back side of a straight or skew chisel can be used for thin, fine shaving as you smooth out rough carving ridges.

Bull nose chisels have a slight arc along the cutting edge with the end points of the edge rounded. This is an excellent tool for any relief carver's tool kit, especially for smoothing work.

V-Gouges

The V-gouge, also called a paring tool, has a crisply angled cutting edge with two straight sides that create a V-shaped cut. The angle of the cutting profile ranges from very tight, narrow angles for fine detailing to wide, open angles for separating one area of a carving from another. The size of the cutting edge also varies from micro V-gouges that have ⅛" (0.3cm)–high cutting sides to ½" (1.3cm)–high sides for mallet work. Most V-gouges found in beginners' tool kits have 90-degree angles.

Sharpening Knives

The leather or synthetic strop used with honing or sharpening compound keeps the sharp, crisp edge developed during the fine stonework pristine. Rouging or sharpening compounds come in a variety of grits and are most often noted by their color: green, red oxide, or yellow.

Any carving kit will need a few basic sharpening stones. Shown to the left in the photo above are a red Japanese water stone with a white ceramic fine stone on top, a ceramic slip strop, and a wood slip strop with yellow stropping compound. To the right are a round white slip stone, a leather strop and red oxide rouge, and a synthetic strop with aluminum oxide compound.

Coarse sharpening stones, which are used to create the bevel along the cutting edge, are graded from 600 grit to 1000 grit and are available in natural stone, manmade stone, and ceramic. Graded from 2000 to 6000 grit, fine sharpening stones create the actual cutting edge.

For round gouges, wide sweep gouges, and bull nose chisels, you will want to use a slip strop or a slip stone, which has premade contours that fit the shape of your gouge.

Safety First

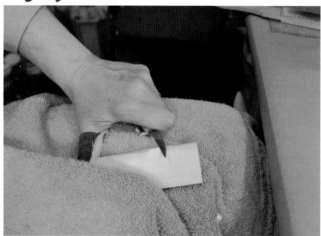

Kevlar carving gloves and thumb protectors can protect your hands from cuts that may occur during any carving session. As shown in the photo (above), a heavyweight terry cloth towel can be used to protect your holding hand and lap.

The most common cause of injury during a woodcarving session is forcing a dull knife blade through the wood. If you find yourself exerting excessive pressure to make a cut, stop! Remove the knife from the wood and resharpen your edge.

Basic Cuts

Whittling Push Cut

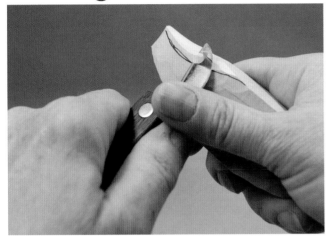

The push cut is made with a bench knife or large chip carving knife. The knife is held at a low angle to the wood with the blade pointed away from your body. The cut is made by pushing the knife blade through the wood.

Whittling Pull Cut

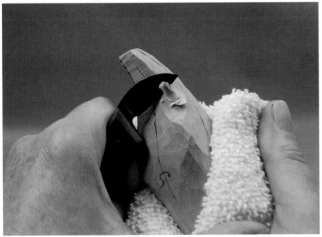

The pull cut is made with the knife blade pointed toward your body. Work at a low angle to the wood. This is also called a paring cut.

Stop Cut

To separate one area of work from another or to create a ledge or shelf in the layers of your work, use a stop cut.

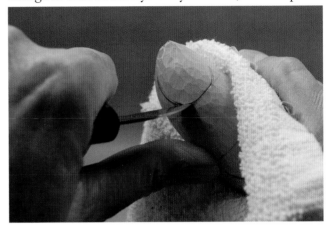

The stop cut is made using two cuts. The first cut is made using the tip or point of the knife, cutting a thin line straight into the wood along the pattern line.

The second cut is made by dropping the bench knife blade to a low angle to the wood. Start the stroke slightly away from the first cut, then slice toward that cut. This will lift a small wedge or sliver of wood on one side of the first cut.

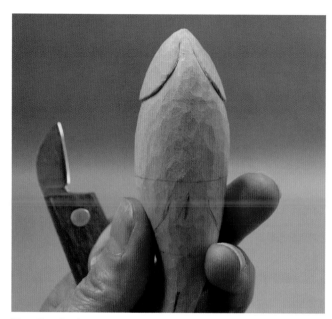

The finished stop cut will have one side of the cut at the original level of the wood and the second side lower.

Rounding-Over Cut

Small, thin cuts are used to round over an angle or edge to create a smooth curve. Hold the knife blade very low to the wood and take small, short strokes. Rounding over may be done using either the push or pull cutting stroke.

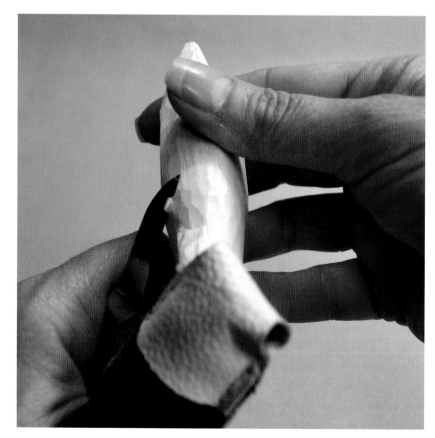

Wood Grain Direction

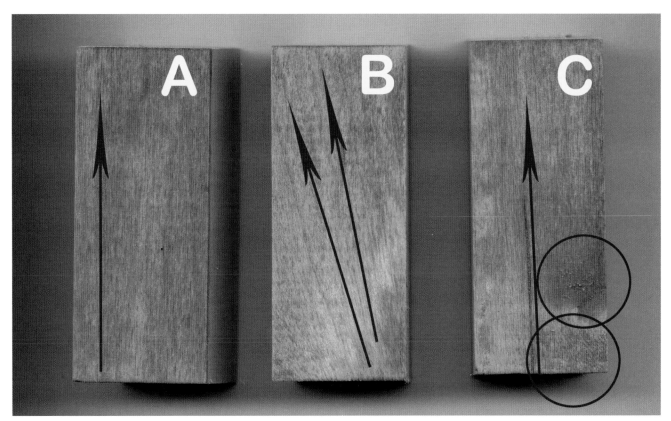

Before you begin any carving, check the grain of the basswood block you will be carving for grain direction and for imperfections that will affect your cuts.

Block A, shown on the left, has nice, even grain lines and is perfect for virtually any use.

Block B, shown middle, has the wood grain running on a diagonal direction across the face of the block. The angle of the grain can throw off your knife cuts and cause excessively thick slivers in your chips. While a carving block with slightly off-center grain can easily be used for a cane topper, I suggest that you set aside any block where the grain runs past 15 degrees of center for use in other projects.

Block C, shown right, has fairly straight grain lines, but shows a large knothole area in the lower right-hand corner. Knotholes are extra-dense areas in the wood and can split out. Do not use a knothole block for facial carving.

Finishing

There are a wide variety of finishes and sealers that you can use on wooden projects. Each has its own specific advantages and disadvantages. Here's a quick look at some of the possible finishes you can use on your cane toppers. Finishes come in four basic chemical types: acrylic or polymer; polyurethane, shellac, or varnish; oil or oil-based; and wax. Acrylic and polyurethane type sealers are available as both brush-on liquids and sprays. Oil, oil-based, and wax finishes are usually applied using a soft, clean cloth.

General Finishing Tips

Preparation is key. Sand and clean before starting any finishing steps. Remove dust with a dry, lint-free cloth. Make sure all glue is dry. Always take time to thoroughly read the label of your sealer or finish, including the application instructions and any cautions or possible hazards with using the product.

It is better to apply several light coats of any finish than to apply one heavy coat. Allow plenty of time between coats for the prior coat to completely dry. All finishes are made to seal the wood from moisture. If you apply a second coat too quickly, you can inadvertently trap the remaining moisture in the first coat under the second coat.

Acrylic

Acrylic and latex sealers leave your work with a smooth, crystal clear finish and are available in both brush-on and spray forms. This type of finish gives a medium-hard surface that is wonderful for brightly colored works.

Advantages: Acrylic sealers dry quickly—within 15 to 20 minutes under dry humidity conditions. You can build up layers of sealer without the sealer becoming cloudy or sticky, which makes an acrylic sealer perfect for projects that require a sealing coat between different colors or paint applications.

Disadvantages: Acrylic sealers have a narrow temperature range, from 50 to 85 degrees Fahrenheit (10 to 30 degrees Celsius). So for very cold or hot weather, use the brush-on form. Acrylic and latex finishes also lay on the wood rather than penetrate the wood grain, meaning that over time the sealer may crack or peel, leaving your work with a scaly, cloudy surface.

I use spray acrylic or latex finishes when I need a quick drying time and when I want a bright, extra-shiny gloss finish.

Polyurethane

Polyurethane sealers leave a very hard finished surface and are often used on floors and furniture that will see hard use. Work in a well-ventilated area and avoid inhaling the fumes. While polyurethanes take a while to dry completely between coats, they do penetrate into the top surface of the wood grain.

Advantages: Leaving a long-lasting finish, polyurethane sealers seldom cloud, crack, or peel with age. The hard nature of this sealer makes it appropriate for any project that will receive hard, continuous use—like a cane topper.

Disadvantages: Because of the thick nature of a polyurethane brush-on sealer, it is easy to accidentally over-apply this finish. Do not carry an excessive amount of sealer in your brush, which can cause the sealer to puddle in the deep crevices. Polyurethane also takes longer to dry between coats than acrylic sealers.

I use a polyurethane brush-on finish as my final coat for any decorative, brightly colored work and for any project that will receive hard use.

Paste Wax

Paste wax, which is floor wax polish, leaves your projects with a wonderful tactile feeling. This finish is easy to use and easy to reapply over the years to refresh the surface of your project.

Advantages: Paste wax can be applied directly to raw wood, over painted surfaces, and even over other sealers as a final sealing coat. It can be used directly at your studio table and under just about any atmospheric condition. Use multiple coats to build up a soft sheen. One can of paste wax will last for years.

Disadvantages: Over time and with constant use, paste wax finishes can wear off your project and may need to be reapplied.

Paste wax is a favorite finish for me for any project that will be held in someone's hand. In my opinion, no other sealer has the soft, inviting feeling of a paste wax finish. I often turn to paste wax for my cane toppers, walking sticks, and chess sets.

Oil

Oil finishes, such as Danish oil, Tung oil, and a boiled linseed oil/turpentine mixture, do not create a hard, solid surface, so you do not lose the feeling and look of the wood and wood grain of your project. Oils penetrate into the

wood itself rather than lie on top of the wood, so they do not leave the plastic or glassy effect of an acrylic or polyurethane sealer.

Boiled linseed oil, mixed half and half with turpentine, is my favorite wood finish for relief carvings, and can be a good choice for cane toppers. The turpentine thins the boiled linseed oil enough that the oil deeply penetrates into the wood grain. That added oil, deep in the wood, helps avoid cupping and warping that can come with time as the wood dries out. I personally love the golden amber tones that this mixture gives to my otherwise quite white and bland basswood projects.

Advantages: Boiled linseed oil mixed with turpentine can be applied at your studio table under most atmospheric conditions. It penetrates the wood quickly and is ready to wipe clean with a dry cotton cloth within 15 minutes. You can build up several coats to create a very soft, satin sheen. This mix is wonderful when you need a temporary finish for your carvings. If you are not sure that your carving is done and may want to set it aside for a while before you add those last detailing steps, a light coating of boiled linseed oil and turpentine will protect the wood, allowing you to return to the carving steps later.

Disadvantages: The primary disadvantage with any oil finish, but especially with boiled linseed oil, is that the rags, brushes, and papers that you use are highly flammable. Immediately after application, place all of the oil rags and papers into a can that is half filled with soapy water. Completely submerge them in the water. Place the can outside, in the shade, away from any buildings until you can dispose of it properly, according to your local laws. The second disadvantage to oil finishes is that they add a golden amber tone to the wood, which will affect any painting steps that you have worked.

Burnishing

You can also finish a wood project without using additional products by burnishing the wood. Using a wood stick that is of a harder wood species than the project itself, firmly rub across the unpainted wood surface. The harder wood stick compresses the wood grain on the surface of the work as well as polishes it, leaving a semi-gloss, smooth sheen on the work. Burnishing is perfect when you want the feeling of the wood to become part of your finished work.

Advantages: Burnishing accents the wood grain and wood feeling of your project without placing a sealing coat between you and the wood. You can return to a burnished project at any time to apply acrylic, polyurethane, wax, or oil finishes.

Disadvantages: Burnishing your wood surface, as with oil sealers, does not protect the wood from moisture or stains.

Planning Your Cane

Answer this set of questions before proceeding with any new cane topper carving so that you can be sure you end up with your desired result. You have learned about each of these things in the previous pages and chapters. If you need a refresher on any item, just flip back through.

1. What type of piece do you want to create?
- A. Cane
- B. Walking stick
- C. Hiking stick
- D. Wizard's wand

2. Where do you want the grip?
- A. On the stick or staff area
- B. On the cane topper
- C. On the joint of the topper and staff

3. How do you want to join the topper to the cane?
- A. Flush cut joint
- B. Plug joint

4. What joinery hardware do you want to use?
- A. Hardwood dowel
- B. All thread rod
- C. Metal hangers or screws

5. How will you accent or hide the joint area?
- A. Hardwood inserts
- B. Cord wraps
- C. Lanyard

6. Do you want to add any extras?
- A. Bags
- B. Pipes
- C. Additional wood
- D. Wire elements
- E. Cane tips
- F. Grips

7. How do you want to finish the cane?
- A. Peeled or partially peeled
- B. With the bark, or sanded bark

8. What finishing product do you want to use?
- A. Oil finish
- B. Spray sealer finish
- C. Paste wax finish
- D. Brush-on finish

Chapter 6: Projects

Now that you have been introduced to all the essential components and techniques of cane topper carving, it's time to try your hand at some projects. In this chapter, you'll get in-depth instructions for carving four interesting toppers: the GI Joe Mushroom, the Wood Spirit, the Tiki, and the Twistie Snake. You'll also get some quick tutorials on additional characters to carve. By the time you've worked through even one or two of the projects in this chapter, you'll be well on your way to being able to carve any topper you set your mind to. Even if you aren't particularly attracted to any of the projects provided here, you should follow along with them, because they are chock full of important tips and tricks for great, clean work.

GI Joe Mushroom Topper: Carving the Planes of the Face

In this project, we will first learn in detail how to approach the carving of a face into a cane topper. At the end, we will transform the carved face into a full-blown character cane topper, the GI Joe Mushroom.

Materials (for basic face carving)

- GI Joe Mushroom pattern (page 139)
- 1¼" x 1¼" x 4" (3.2 x 3.2 x 10cm) basswood block for face
- Bench knife or large chip carving knife
- V-gouge
- Large round gouge
- Graphite paper
- Additional materials to complete the GI Joe Mushroom listed on page 75

Facial Features

With not a lot of complicated cutting, we will be able to create many different facial features in our cane topper.

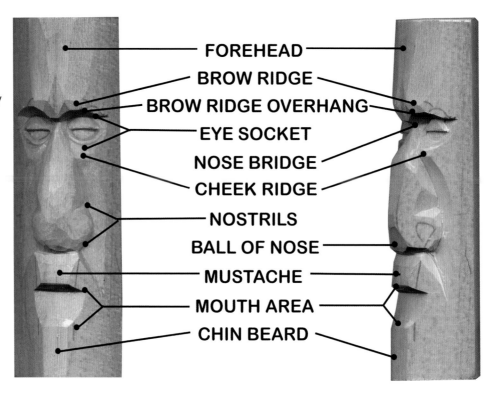

FOREHEAD

BROW RIDGE

BROW RIDGE OVERHANG

EYE SOCKET

NOSE BRIDGE

CHEEK RIDGE

NOSTRILS

BALL OF NOSE

MUSTACHE

MOUTH AREA

CHIN BEARD

Progressive Steps Preview

Here you can see the general progression we will follow to achieve the final carved face. It's not intimidating!

Carving the Planes of the Face

1 Work on a corner edge.

This specific style of face carving works off the corner edge of the basswood block. That right angle area automatically sets the sides of the triangular shape of the nose.

Try this: Place the flat of your hands on the sides of your face so that your palms touch your ears and your fingertips touch at the tip of your nose. Note how the angle between your hands is more or less a right angle. Working off the corner of the basswood block uses that 90-degree angle in the wood to create the same angle that your hands found in your face.

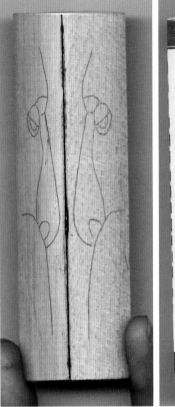 

2 Transfer the pattern.

Make a copy of the pattern (page 139). Resize the pattern to fit your particular basswood block. The pattern shown in the steps is sized for a 1¼" x 1¼" x 4" (3.2 x 3.2 x 10cm) block.

Cut a piece of graphite paper the same size as your pattern paper. Lay the graphite under the pattern paper with the shiny side down, dull side to the pattern paper. Fold the pattern along the dotted line. Center the dotted line between the two faces along the front corner of your block. Tape into place. Then, using a pen or pencil, trace along all the pattern lines to transfer the graphite pattern to the block.

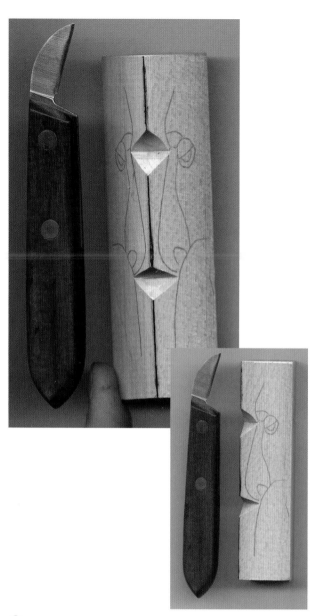

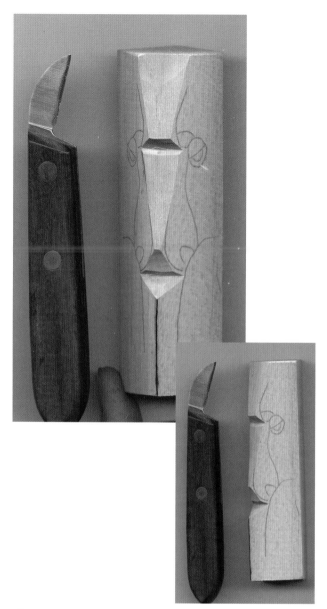

3 Cut the nose bridge angles.

The first set of cuts establishes the top of the nose at the nose bridge and the bottom of the nose at the nose ball.

This is a simple push stroke, cut into the corner. Make one slice, at a 45-degree angle, just below the nose bridge line of the pattern, pushing up toward the forehead.

Turn the block upside down and make a second cut, starting just above the nose bridge line, slicing down into the first cut. Repeat these two cuts to open the double triangle wedge.

4 Slant the nose and forehead.

Establish the slant of the nose by cutting from the nose ball tip toward the nose bridge cut. Taper the forehead away from the nose bridge.

Tip: I prefer to use several shallow, thin cuts to create a slant in the wood as the one cut along the center ridge of nose. Small cuts give you more control over the knife and over the angle and depth of the cut area. Trying to take out the wood for the nose slant in one deep cut can cause the knife blade to bind up under the thickness of the wood sliver.

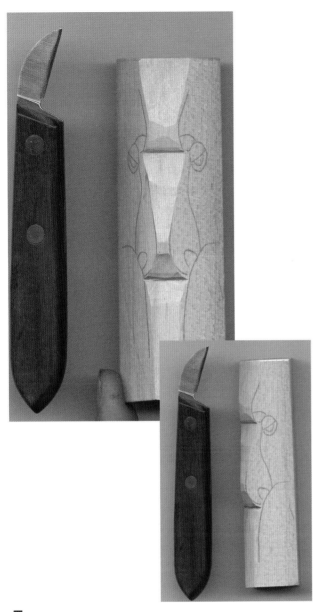

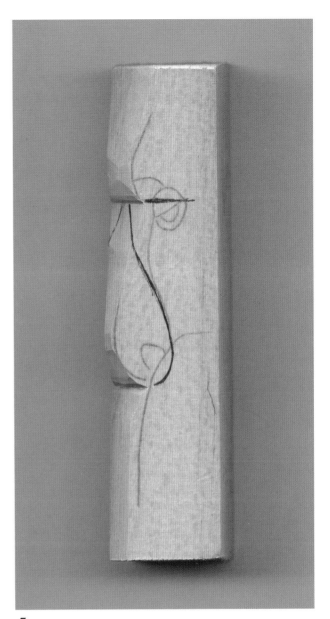

5 Round over the brow ridge and mustache area.

The brow ridge, the area above the nose bridge at the lowest point in the forehead, is rounded over slightly with a few bench knife cuts.

Taper the mustache and beard area below the nose ball wedge cut. This area is a straight line cut, or can flair forward at the bottom of the block to create an extra-full beard area.

Tip: Run your finger down the center of your face, starting at your hairline and ending at the bottom edge of your chin. Steps 3 through 5 have set the center facial line and planes that your finger just traced.

6 Mark the brow ridge and outer edge of the nose.

With a pencil, mark a straight line on the sides of the block along the center cut line of the nose ridge wedge. This line marks the bottom edge of the brow ridge overhang above the eyes.

With a pencil, mark the outer edge of the nose, starting at the nose bridge and ending at the nose ball tip.

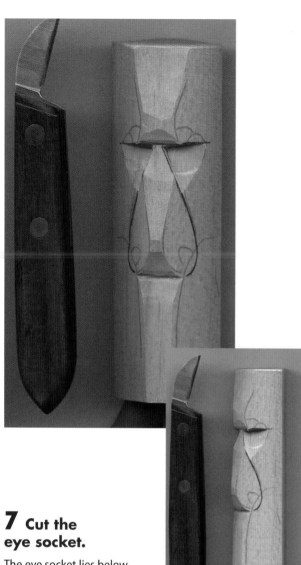

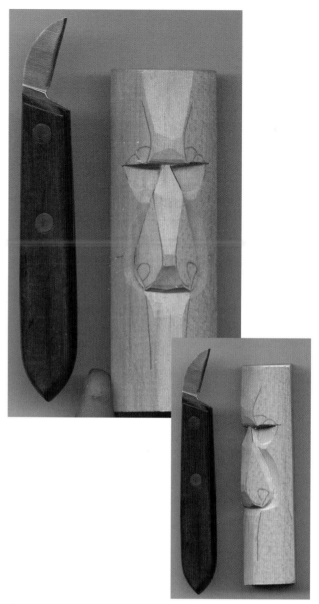

7 Cut the eye socket.

The eye socket lies below the bridge of the nose, and the eyebrow line lies on a 90-degree angle to the nose.

Make a stop cut along the edge of the nose, angling the tip during the cut to create the 90-degree line for the eye socket.

Make a stop cut along the brow ridge pencil line.

Using a push cut, lift a triangle slice for the eye socket. Make the cut from the cheek area working toward the brow ridge. You can re-cut the stop cuts and repeat the push cut to slowly lower the eye socket.

Note in the side view that the push cut into the brow ridge creates a natural curve to the triangle, with the lower edge of the curve becoming the top of the cheek.

8 Cut the cheek crease.

To separate the sides of the nose from the cheek area, create a stop cut along the nose side pattern line. This cut is at a 90-degree angle to the face.

Cut along the cheek area with the bench knife to create a V-shaped crease line. This line begins about ⅛" (0.3cm) or more from the bottom edge of the eye socket.

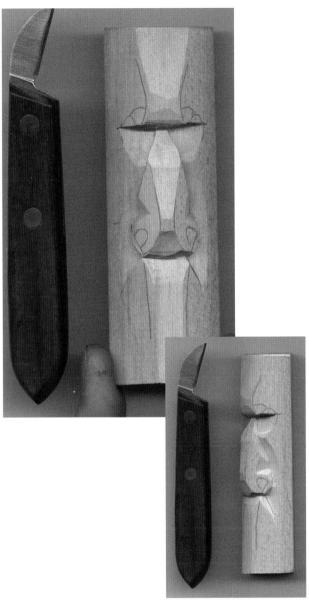

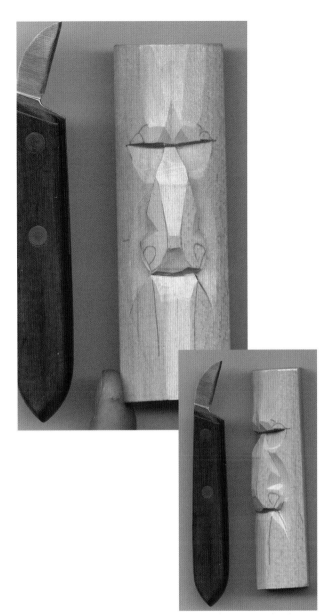

9 V-cut the nostrils.

To separate the nostrils from the main trunk of the nose, cut a V-shaped wedge along the top of the nostril pattern line. Cut a second V-shaped wedge to separate the top side edges of the mustache from the face.

Tip: Run your finger down the side of your nose, starting at the nose bridge and ending at the bottom of the nostril. As your finger moves, you will feel an outward curve in the nose above the nostril. The center of the bulge is where the nose bone stops. The V-shaped cuts done in this step set the top of the nostril and create the shape of the bulge along the side of the nose.

10 Create the forehead crease.

Cut a V-shaped diamond at the center of the brow ridge in the bottom edge of the forehead. Round over the bottom edge of the forehead to begin the curve of the brow ridge.

Tip: If you run your finger down the center of your forehead to the nose bridge, you may feel a small trough in the skull in the forehead area. You will not feel a deep, distinct V-shaped diamond like the one cut in this step. As a person ages, the hairs in the eyebrows grow in length, creating a bushier eyebrow effect. The V-shaped diamond creates the depth to imply bushy eyebrows.

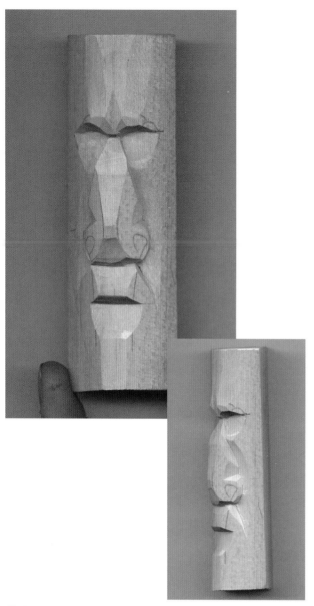

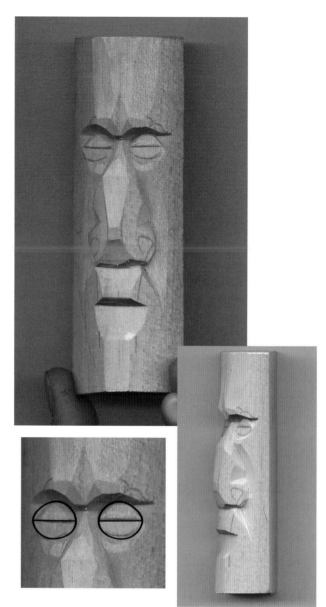

11 Cut the mouth wedge.

Cut the wedge for the mouth below the bottom edge of the mustache. The wedge curves deeper into the face, working from the top of the chin into the bottom mustache edge.

Tip: At this point in the carving, all of the facial planes have been worked and have set the depth in the face for each individual area. Even though the proportions for each facial plane area may change, all faces can begin with these basic cuts. How you work the shaping and detailing in each area determines the unique characteristics and personality of each face.

12 Set the depth of the eyes.

Using a pencil, mark a wide, leaf-shaped line for the eyes in the eye socket area. Draw a line through the center of this leaf shape. The line divides the top eyelid from the open eyeball area of the face.

Working in the upper eye socket area, cut along the outline of the upper eyelid. Cut small triangles in the socket area to give the eyelid a raised effect.

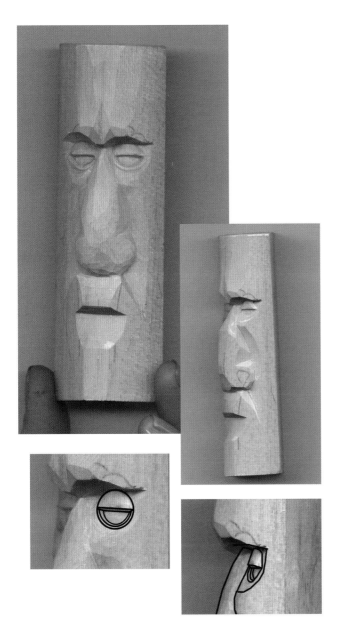

13 Shape the eyelids.

To define the lower eyeball area, use a V-gouge to cut two V-trough lines. One line is cut on the leaf-shaped pencil line and becomes the inner edge of the lower eyelid. The second line is 1/16" (0.2cm) below the first and defines the lower edge of the lower eyelid.

Round over the upper eyelid, the eyeball area in the lower portion of the eye, and the nose. Lightly shape the cheek areas.

14 Round the nose.

The mustache is shaped to become a smooth curve just below the nose. Since the mustache is created in the face with hair, however, it has no sharp-edge outline. Gently blend the top edge of the mustache into the lower cheek area.

Hold your bench knife at a low angle to the wood and shave along the sides and ball of the nose. A low angle to the blade allows you to remove very thin slices of wood.

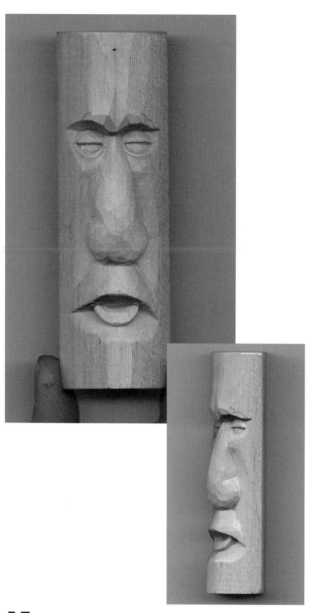

15 Cut the lower lip.

Using a pencil, draw a half-circle line for the lower edge of the lower lip. Stop cut along this line with your bench knife and cut along the chin area to give the lip a raised effect.

Draw a second half-circle line in the mouth area ⅛" (0.3cm) above the first. This marks the top edge of the lower lip. Stop cut along this line and lower the wood inside the mouth.

16 Round the cheeks.

Using the bench knife at a low angle to the wood, give the entire face a general shaping using small, short cutting strokes.

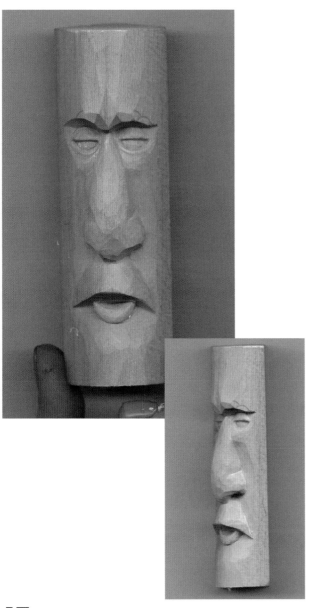

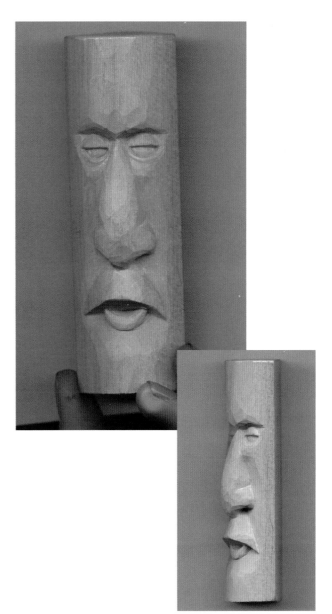

17 Shape the lower nose.

The bottom edge of the nose includes three small ball shapes: the bottom of the left nostril, the center ball of the nose, and the bottom of the right nostril.

Cut along the bottom edge of each nostril to taper the nose into a V-shape with the ball of the nose at the tip of the V.

Tip: Place your finger and thumb over the nostrils of your nose. You can feel the center bottom edge of your nose between your fingers. The outer edges of your nostrils are slightly higher than the center lower point of your nose. The ball of your nose lies above your fingers.

18 Cut the nostril openings.

A large round gouge is used to cut into the nose at the bottom of each nostril to create the nose opening.

Place the cutting edge of your gouge where you want the nostril. Gently rock the edge of the gouge into the wood, making a straight cut into the nostril area.

Use your bench knife to trim any excess wood left from the round gouge cut.

Give the face a final shaping and cleaning. You are ready to add hair detailing and wrinkles as desired using your V-gouge.

Creating the GI Joe Mushroom

Any basic face can be modified to create a new personality. Here, we will look at how to create the GI Joe Mushroom out of the basic face we just learned to carve (or any face you have carved). This particular character was carved in an exaggerated style with an extra-long nose, small eyes, extra-deep eye sockets, and a small, straight mustache. The piece is worked in four separate basswood blocks: one for the face, one for the cap, and two for the background mushrooms.

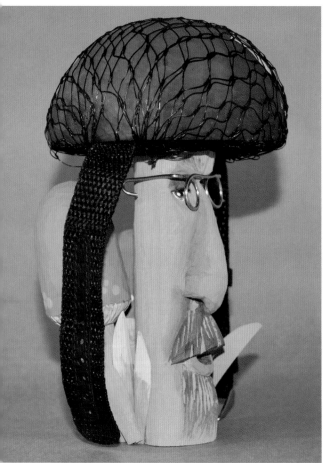

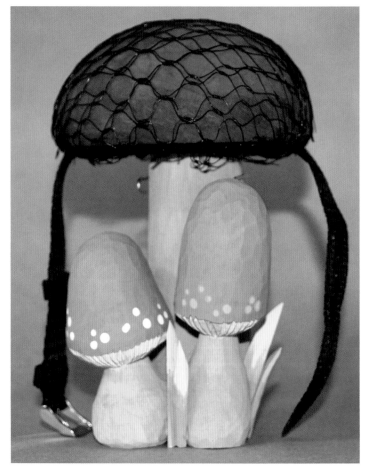

Materials

- Completed GI Joe face carving (see page 63)
- 3" x 3½" x 2" (7.5 x 9 x 5cm) basswood block for cap
- 1½" x 1½" x 4" (3.8 x 3.8 x 10cm) block for large mushroom
- 1½" x 1½" x 3" (3.8 x 3.8 x 7.5cm) block for small mushroom
- Leftover wood scraps from carving the face
- Bench knife or large chip carving knife
- V-gouge
- Large round gouge
- Carpenter's wood glue
- Graphite paper
- 320-grit sandpaper
- 8" (20.5cm) square of brown craft paper or paper bag
- Soft, lint-free cloth
- Assorted acrylic craft paints
- Assorted soft-bristle paintbrushes
- Black plastic netting (such as from a vegetable bag)
- Large-eyed needlepoint needle
- Black crochet cotton thread, size 10
- Nylon watchband
- Superglue
- 16-gauge copper jewelry wire
- Round-nosed pliers
- Polyurethane or acrylic spray sealer

1 After the basic steps for the face carving have been completed, use a V-gouge to cut the detail V-trough lines in the mustache, the beard, and eyebrows.

2 Carve the mushroom cap using a bench knife and a round gouge. Create a bowl-shaped curve on the inside of the cap using a large round gouge. Use a V-gouge to cut the ribbing lines inside the cap. Use carpenter's wood glue to secure the cap to the top of the facial piece. (For more information on attaching mushroom caps, see page 76.)

3 Carve the small mushrooms from the remaining basswood blocks. Cut the bases of the mushrooms at an angle to tip the caps away from the facial piece. (For more information on attaching additional mushrooms, see page 76.)

4 Cut blades of grass from the rough-out chip scraps left over from carving the face.

5 Lightly sand the entire carving using 320-grit sandpaper. Crumple a piece of brown kraft paper or paper bag and rub it all over the carving; this will give an extra-fine sanding to the wood. Remove any dust with a soft, lint-free cloth.

6 Paint the carved mushrooms as desired using acrylic craft paints.

7 Using carpenter's wood glue, secure the mushrooms to the back of the facial piece. You can flatten one side of the mushrooms where they touch the facial piece, using your bench knife, to create a larger gluing surface. Glue the blades of grass into place. Allow the glue to dry overnight.

8 The helmet netting is made from black plastic netting used as a vegetable bag. Cut the netting into two large circles that are 8" (20.5cm) in diameter. Lay one circle on top of the other and work both as one unit. Using a large-eyed needlepoint needle and black crochet cotton, thread the crochet cotton through the netting holes along the outside edges of the circles. Leave 4" (10cm) to 5" (12.5 cm) of extra thread at each end of the circle.

9 Lay the netting circle over the mushroom cap and tighten the crochet cotton to gather the circle under the edges of the mushroom cap. Tie the thread ends in a knot to hold the netting in place. Clip the excess thread.

10 A nylon watchband is used to create the chin straps for the helmet. Superglue the watchband pieces to the underside of the mushroom cap. Allow the glue to set for one hour. While it is setting, create the glasses out of copper wire. (For more information on creating wire glasses, see page 46).

11 Finish the carving with several light coats of polyurethane or acrylic spray sealer.

Attaching Caps and Small Mushrooms

Wood spirit mushrooms can be created as single-piece carvings, or by carving the cap separate from the stem (or facial piece), then gluing the cap into place. For a two-piece mushroom like this, you will want to cut an insert area in the cap to receive the top portion of the mushroom stem. Mushroom caps come in three basic shapes—flat caps, bowl-shaped caps, and balloon-shaped caps. Work the carving steps to cut and shape both the facial piece and cap in whatever shape you desire.

To attach the cap, place the flat top of the facial piece into position against the bottom of the cap. Draw around the stem top with a pencil, marking the insert outline on the bottom of the cap. Use a round gouge and bench knife to cut an indented area in the bottom of the cap, approximately ¼" (0.5cm) to ⅜" (1cm) deep, to receive the stem. Sand both the facial piece top and the insert area in the mushroom cap using 220-grit and 320-grit sandpaper. Remove any excess dust. After the insert is cut and sanded, add any detailing lines for the mushroom cap ribbing using a V-gouge. Finally, attach the two pieces using carpenter's glue.

Small additional mushrooms can also be carved and added around the base of a larger wood spirit mushroom. These accent mushrooms can be left plain or can have their own unique faces.

Carve the small accent mushroom from a small basswood block. Cut the bottom edge of the small mushroom to angle its cap away from the stem of the larger mushroom, ensuring that the two pieces will be able to fit together snugly. Position the small mushroom against the base of the larger one. Mark where the sides of the two mushrooms will connect. Then use your bench knife to cut a flat plane in both mushrooms at the joint area. This will give you more gluing surface. Attach the small mushroom to the larger stem using carpenter's glue.

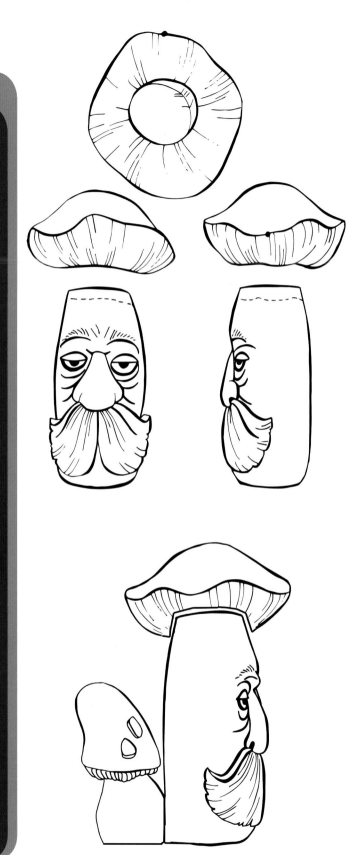

Wood Spirit Topper

This wood spirit is full of interesting details, from the texture of his beard to the decorative beads in his mustache to his expressive face. Follow along as we carve this piece in detail.

We will be using basswood again for this project because of its useful features discussed previously. Remember, once you are comfortable with basswood, you can try carving on different woods, too. Remember also to make sure you start any carving project with knives that are nice and sharp, and sharpen them as you work as well. I always finish a carving session with a quick sharpening of my tools, which means that I can begin the next session with nicely sharpened edges.

Note: For this project, the instructions will include free-handing the pattern on the block. If you prefer, you can transfer the pattern to the block and follow it as you go instead.

Materials

- Wood Spirit pattern (page 138)
- 1½" x 1½" x 12" (3.8 x 3.8 x 30.5cm) basswood block
- Bench knife
- Small round gouge
- Large round gouge
- V-gouge
- Small skew chisel
- Pencil
- 220- and 320-grit sandpaper
- Old toothbrush
- Soft, lint-free cloth
- Assorted acrylic craft paints
- Assorted soft-bristle paintbrushes
- Polyurethane or acrylic spray sealer

Working the Basic Face Shape

The placement of the three horizontal lines in step 1 determines the length of the facial features. If you create a short space between the brow ridge line and the nose line, you create a short nose, whereas a long distance between the lines will create a long nose.

1 Working on one corner of the basswood block, mark three lines. The top line will become the guide for the brow ridge, the middle line denotes the bottom of the nose, and the bottom line shows the bottom of the mouth area. My brow ridge line falls 1½" (3.8cm) from the top of the block. The bottom nose line is 2½" (6.3cm) from the top of the block, and the mouth line is at 3¼" (8.3cm) below the top of the block.

2 Work the brow ridge first. You are going to cut a double wedge between the brow ridge line and the nose line to create the slope of the nose. The first cut of the wedge marks where the bridge of the nose will be. Using your bench knife, begin the slice by angling the knife from the brow ridge line toward the nose line. Keep the slant tight to the brow ridge line.

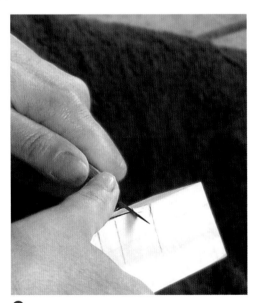

3 Turn the block upside down and make a second sloping cut into the first. This second cut creates the slope of the nose and is shallower in angle than the first cut. Note that I start this second cut in the middle of the space between the brow ridge line and the nose line.

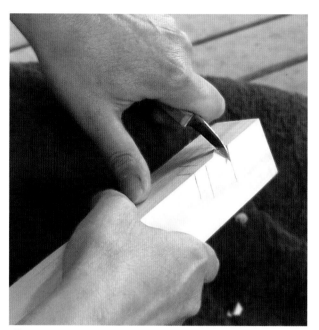

4 Repeat these two cuts until the wedge is approximately ½" (1.5cm) deep. As you work the wedge, allow about one third of the space below the wedge to remain uncarved. This area will become the bulb of the nose.

5 In this photo, you can see the depth of the nose bridge and the slope of the nose.

6 Using a pencil, mark two angled lines, one for each side of the nose. Within these lines you will be carving the nose, nose bulb, and nostrils.

The deeper you carve the initial wedge, the deeper your wood spirit's nose will be. The space that you leave below the wedge determines the size of the nose bulb. So, shallow wedges create shallow noses, and allowing a large space below the wedge creates a large nose bulb.

7 Next, carve out a triangle chip to create the cheek area beside the nose. Using your bench knife in an upright position, create a stop cut along the pencil line.

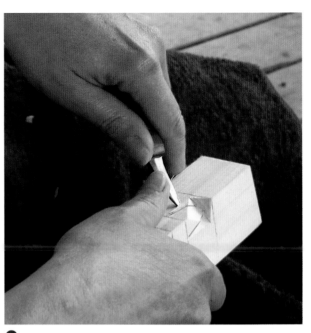

8 Starting at the lower edge of the stop cut, make a slice to the brow ridge wedge. With this cut, the knife blade is dropped to a right angle to the nose.

9 The third side of the triangle is along the brow ridge line. Lay the knife blade in the angle of the brow ridge wedge and pull a stop cut.

10 Here you can see the cheek area created by cutting out this triangle.

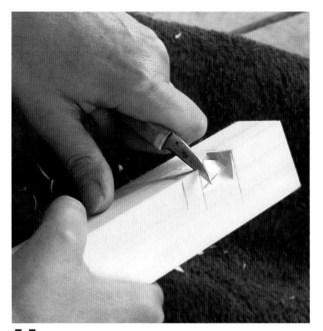

11 The bottom of the nose is established exactly the way you created the brow ridge wedge. The first cut is straight into the wood, and the second is slanted up from the mouth line.

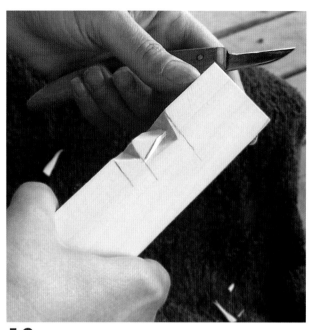

12 You can see the slanted wedge that now establishes the bottom of the nose. Note that the bottom of the nose is not carved as deeply into the wood as the corners or nostril areas.

13 Because the mouth lies deeper in the face than the tip of the nose, the bottom nose wedge is lengthened with a cut starting below the mouth line.

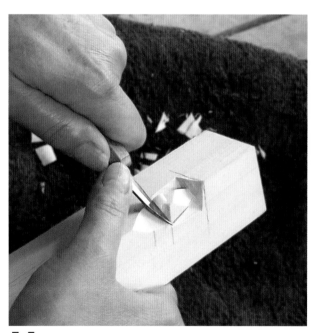

14 Arch this cut as you work. The cut ends at the nose bottom.

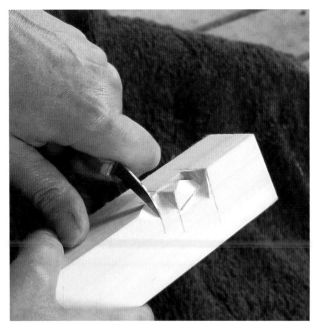

15 The bottom edge of the lower lip is created next. Use your bench knife to make a small wedge under the mouth line.

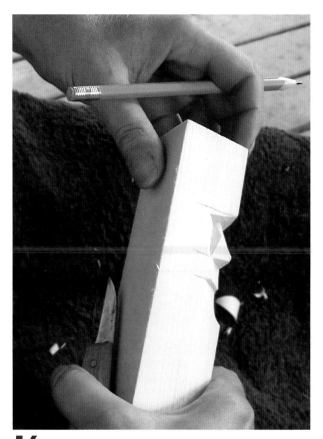

16 At this point you should have a clear brow ridge, nose triangle, bottom edge to the nose, and upper lip line.

17 Begin reducing the extra wood above the brow ridge to create a flat plane for the forehead.

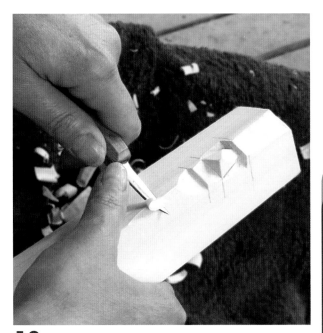

18 Reduce some of the excess below the mouth line. This area will become the beard.

Facial Design Tips

- A wider and deeper brow ridge allows room for heavy, thick eyebrows.

- A greater distance between the brow ridge line and nose line makes room for an extra-long nose.

- The slant of the nose line cut determines if your wood spirit has a downward hooked nose or an upturned nose.

- The distance between the nose and mouth line will decide if your wood spirit will have a small, narrow mustache or deep, flowing mustache.

- The slant of the eye wedge cuts (steps 7–10) at the brow line decides the emotion of your wood spirit. Upward slants become happy or angry and downward slants are sad.

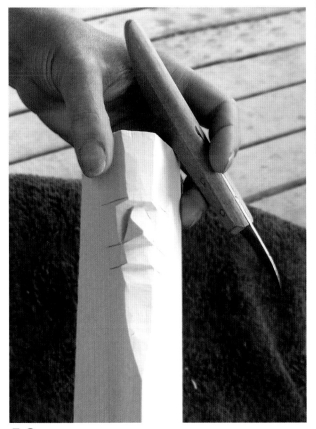

19 At this point, you have created the basic planes of the face and created the positions of the brow ridge, nose, and mustache area.

Carving the Eyes

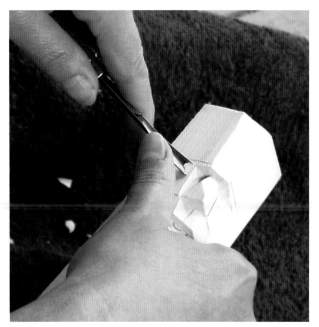

20 The hollow of the eye is created using a large round gouge. The size of this cut determines the size of the eye. Larger gouge strokes create larger eyes. The angle of this cut also decides the slant, upward or downward, that the eyes will have. If this cut is made slanting down from the nose, your wood spirit will appear sad. If the slant moves upward from the nose into the brow area, your wood spirit will become angry. A double-wide gouge mark will make your wood spirit happy or surprised.

21 Here you can see the finished eye hollows.

22 Mark the outside lines of the eyes with a pencil. Pencil in the mustache at the same time.

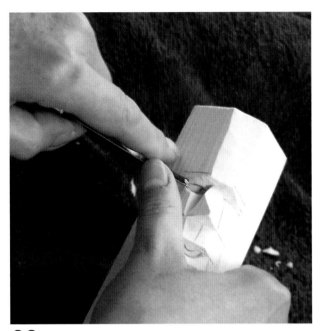

23 Use your V-gouge to cut along the pencil lines for both the upper and lower eyelids.

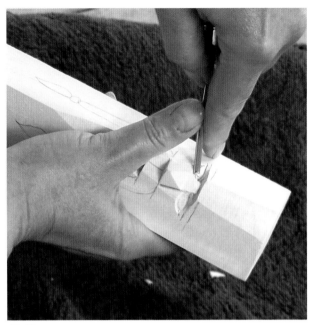

24 Because the lower eyelid curves more sharply than the upper one, this cut can be made in two strokes, working from the center out toward the eye corners.

25 Use a skew chisel to lower the eye inside the V-gouge lines.

26 With the bench knife, crisp the corners of the eye.

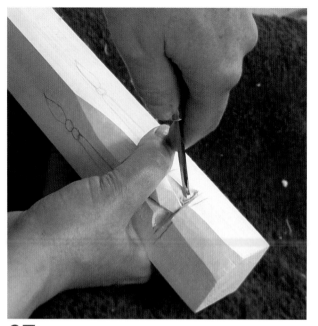

27 Find the center of the eye and make a pencil mark. Use a medium round gouge to create the iris. Push the round gouge into the eye at an upward angle. You may need to roll the gouge to create a large enough circle area. You want a half-circle cut that lies in the upper section of the eye.

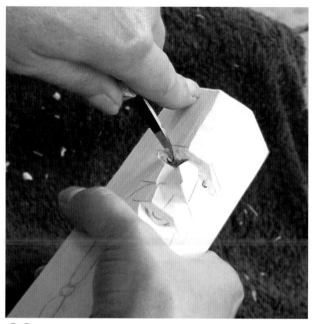

28 Use your bench knife to free the round gouge cut. Shave out the top of the gouge cut so that it is even with the brow area above it. The opening in the mouth is done in the same way as the eye iris.

You create several advantages for yourself by cutting the iris with the gouge. First, the iris of the eye is an opening that appears black. The round gouge cut makes that exact type of deep, shadowed opening in your wood spirit's eye. Second, the gouge can create a wonderfully round opening easier than you can cut it freehand.

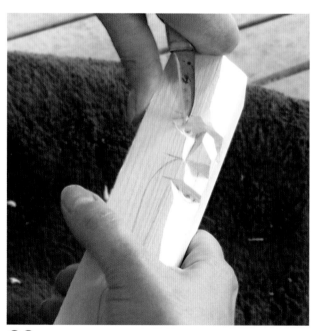

29 The bottom of the brow ridge is shaped next with the bench knife. Gently roll over this area.

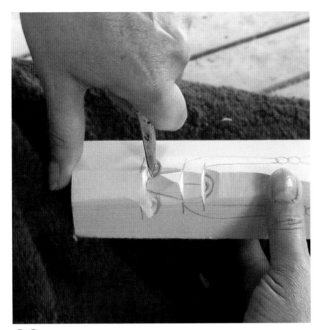

30 Use the bench knife to cut a small chip from the nose corner of the eye. This point should be lower than the rest of the eye.

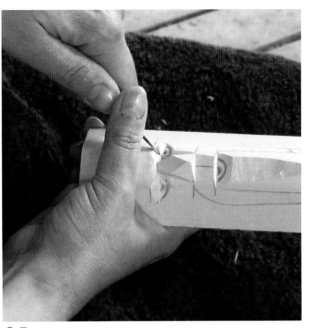

31 Starting at the center of the eye, in the brow area, arch the brow into a half-circle. The photo here shows the finished cuts. Arch the second eyebrow area, again working from the center toward the outside of the face.

32 Roll over the brow above the nose bridge using the bench knife.

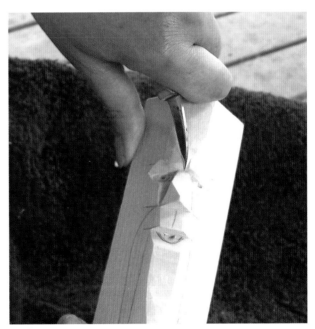

33 Cut two small V shapes to create wrinkles in the brow above the nose.

Shaping the Nose

34 Use a pencil line to mark the nostril areas on the nose. Notice that the nose will be slightly wider above the nostrils.

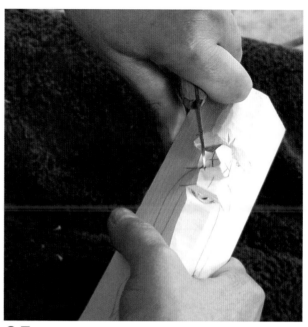

35 Separate the side of the nostrils from the cheek area. Keep your knife vertical to the wood block.

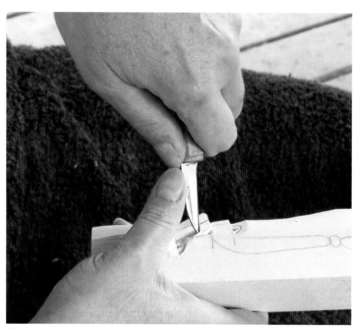

36 Make three cuts above the nostril to free a small triangle from the nose area. This is at the top of the nostrils.

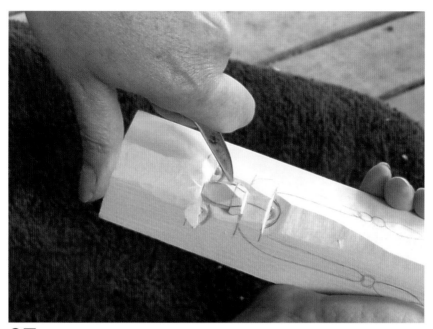

37 Use your bench knife to clean any small slivers of wood on the cheek left over from defining the top of the nostril.

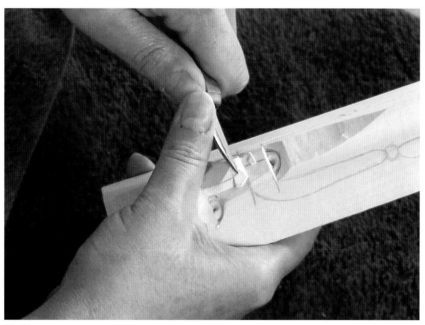

38 Roll over the tip of the nose area.

Shaping the Facial Planes

39 You want to drop the cheek area of the face where it touches the top of the mustache. This area is dropped just above the depth of the eyes.

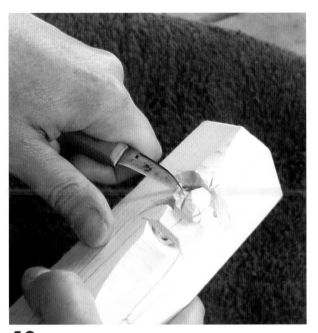

40 There is a sharp edge down the center of the cheek that is next flattened.

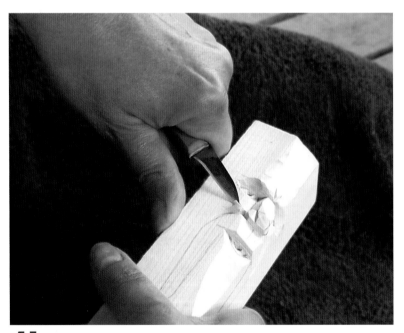

41 Take a moment to smooth out the cheeks, rolling this area away from the nose toward the unworked corner of the block.

42 Roll over the top of the cheek where it meets the eye socket.

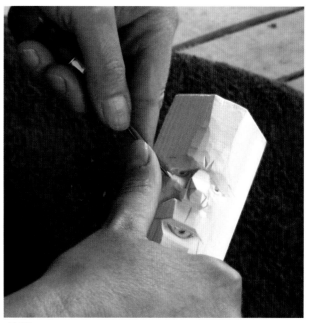

43 Use a V-gouge just below the eye to create a wrinkle or bag.

44 The V-gouge is also used above the mustache to create a smile wrinkle.

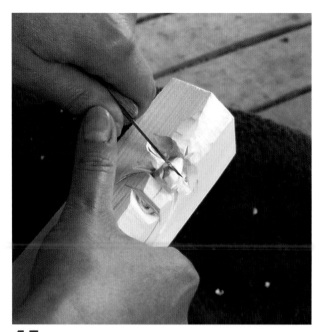

45 Round over the sides of the nose. The nose is narrowest at the bridge, then widens near the middle area. It then narrows slightly where the nostrils are joined. To create a bulb on the end of the nose, shave the center ridge of the nose above the nostril area. This is a gently arched cut.

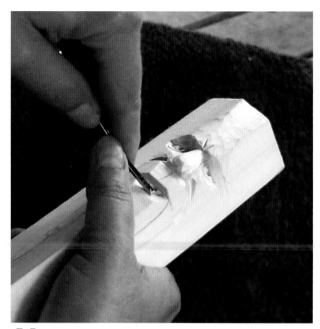

46 Along the bottom lip line, use a V-gouge to separate the lip from the beard area.

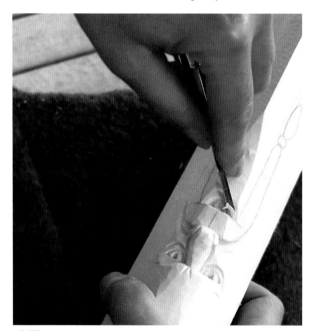

47 Because this is such a tightly curved line, it may be easiest to make this cut using two strokes, each working from the center out. Round over the lip.

Adding Wrinkles

At this point you have finished carving the basic face of your wood spirit. If you want to, now is the best time to add additional wrinkles and aging details. Extra wrinkles and bags can be added under the eyes. As the wrinkle lines move down the face toward the mustache, they become more widely spaced. Wrinkles begin near the nose and fade away as they reach the outer side of the face. Wrinkles can also be added to the forehead area above the brow. Straight-line forehead wrinkles add age to your wood spirit. Wrinkles carved in a V pattern give the impression of anger. If you arch the wrinkles from the center of the forehead down toward the eye corner, the wood spirit will look worried. Just above the bulb of the nose you can also add a few small wrinkles. This will make the bulb area look larger and give it more emphasis.

Adding Hair

The style of hair that you give your wood spirit greatly affects his personality. Wild, unkempt hair that flows into the beard and mustache areas is wonderful when used on a walking stick or cane, as it implies a spirit of freedom. You may choose to add hair above the eyes, or you may wish your wood spirit to be bald. Mustaches can easily be made into braids and twists with bead and feather decorations for a pagan-style wood spirit.

There are five areas of hair to consider:

- Forehead hair or scalp hair above the face
- Back hair that flows from the spirit's temples to the back of the carving
- Mustaches
- Beards
- The small beard area under the lower lip

There are several ways that you can accent your hair areas:

- Feathers can be added to ponytails and mustaches with a hint of leather.
- Single beads or stacks of beads can be positioned in long hair strands.
- Braiding can be created within the beard or mustache area.
- Any strand of hair can be twisted.

This particular wood spirit will have a little bit of every style of hair, so that as you begin to develop your own style of wood spirit, you can incorporate the areas of hair that will most greatly impact your carving and create the effect you desire.

48 Mark a pencil guideline for the lip beard.

49 Use your V-gouge along the pencil guidelines for the two sides of the mustache and the bottom edge of the lip beard to separate these areas from the background wood.

50 Below the lip beard, round over the rest of the front corner of the block.

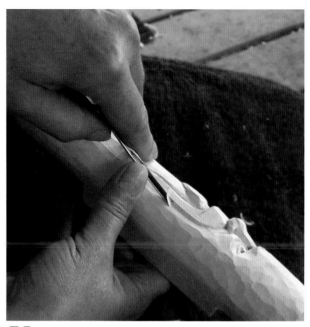

51 Use the V-gouge to define the mustache area. Take the V-gouge into the corner area between the mustache and goatee. This point should be fairly deep.

52 Notice in this photo how the corner points of the goatee are deepest, the next level is the beard, and the mustache stands as the tallest of the hair areas.

53 Round over the mustache and goatee with your bench knife.

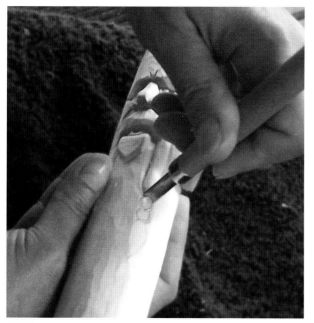

54 Making very round beads is easy using a medium-sized round gouge. Hold the gouge on its profile and roll it between your fingertips to cut the circle.

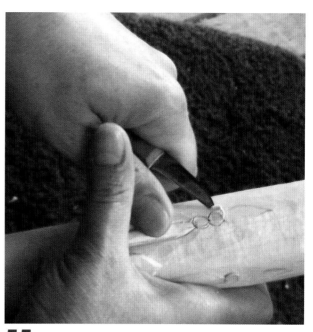

55 Drop the background surrounding the bead circle. Shave this area out level with your previous round-over work.

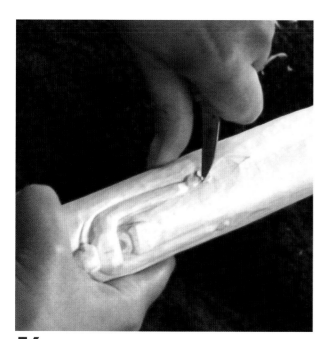

56 Roll over the bead and, if necessary, crisp the separation line between the two beads.

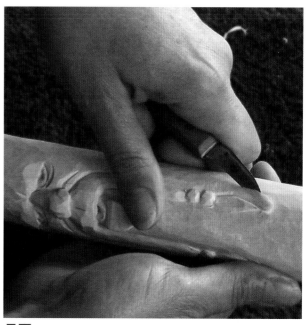

57 Define the bottom of the mustache with the V-gouge. Drop the surrounding background wood with your bench knife and shave it smooth.

58 Round over the goatee. Drop the point of the goatee slightly so that the goatee directly under the lip is higher than where the goatee begins to blend into the beard.

59 Use a pencil to mark where you want your ponytail to fall. The ponytail hair starts at the cheek area of the face. As you mark this area, drop the ponytail hair down from the cheeks, then curve it up into the bead at the center back.

60 Create the ponytail bead exactly as you did the mustache beads using a large round gouge. Free the ponytail hair from the surrounding background wood using the V-gouge and bench knife. You will need to drop the background area captured within the ponytail quite a bit to bring it even with the remaining background.

61 Roll over the ponytail and bead. Since you allowed extra wood for the ponytail work, you can make this area raised fairly high from the surrounding wood.

V-Gouging the Hair Details

Braiding

It is during steps 51–61 that you would do the basic carving for braided hair. Braided hair strands are treated exactly as you have treated the mustache and ponytail. Each part of the braid would first be V-gouged to define it from the surrounding wood. The surrounding wood is then shaved and smoothed out. Finally, each section of the braid is rounded over.

Hair Direction

The hair features for this particular wood spirit fall straight down from the face. However, hair, especially mustaches, can take several shapes and directions. Upturned mustaches can be created that roll up into a half-circle toward the eye. Wide, fan-shaped mustaches can cover the face from the center of the cheeks, then roll down to the beard area. Beards can start at the lower lip, then fan out into a wide bushy Santa Claus–style beard.

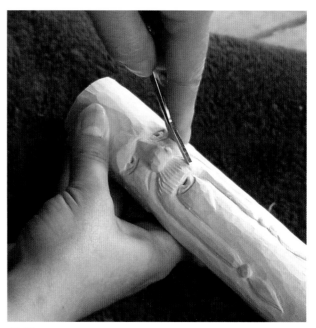

62 The V-gouge is the tool used to create the texturing in each hair section. Heavy cuts create divisions between sections of hair, whereas light cuts create the look of fine individual hairs. Begin your detailing with the mustache. Because this area rolls over tightly, the V-gouge cuts are done in two strokes. The first stroke goes from the center up into the nose, and the second goes from the center down toward the beard.

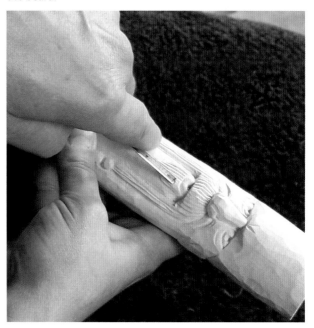

63 Work on the goatee next, with the V-gouge cuts coming together at the point of the goatee.

This is a good place to return to the subject of safety during any carving session. As you work the V-gouge strokes for the hair texture, you will be working over a tightly curved surface and you will be changing the direction of your cut as you work. Because the V-gouge cuts do not go deeply into the wood, the gouge can easily and quickly slip out and slide across your work. Take extra precaution as you work the V-gouge steps, and pay extra attention to the position of your holding hand. If necessary, wrap the basswood inside a terry cloth towel so that your holding hand is covered with the cloth. Most of my own injuries occur during the V-gouge stage.

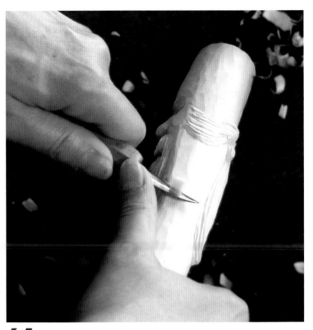

64 Take time to carefully smooth out any rough spots before you begin the V-gouge work in a particular area. The smoother the surface, the easier the V-gouge strokes will move across the wood.

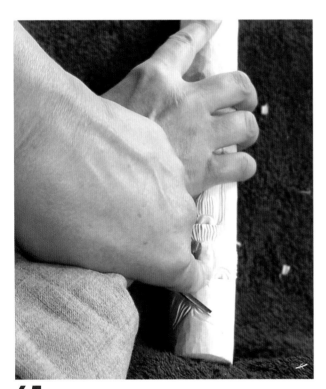

65 The hair above the forehead was not contoured during the earlier carving steps. This hair lies on the same level as the brow ridge. Use just a few cuts to create this section of hair. The hair along the temples is created with just a few downward curved V-gouge cuts.

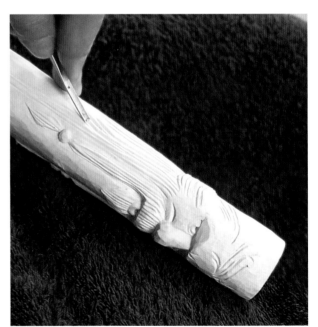

66 The hair along the sides of the face is made of long, flowing V-gouge lines. Make these cuts varied in length, some very long and some very short.

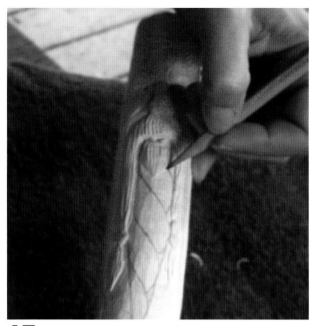

67 Inside the beard area, use a pencil to establish the outside edges of the beard and the twist sections.

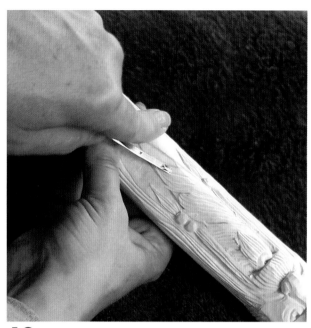

68 The twists are created using an S-shaped line. Start at the bottom of each twist, cut upward, and then roll the cut to the opposite side of the twist.

69 At this point, the carving on your wood spirit is complete. Brush either an old toothbrush or a brass wire brush over the entire work to remove many of the fine wood fibers that remain. Follow this with a light sanding using 220-grit or finer sandpaper. Remove the sanding dust with either a soft, lint-free cloth or a dusting brush. Take some time to double-check your carving. Look for areas that may need a little extra smoothing, detailing, or cleanup.

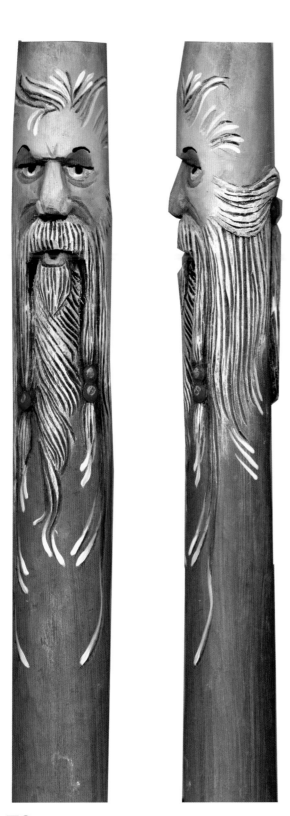

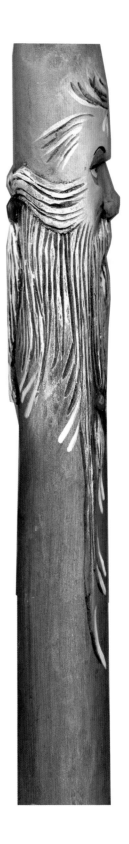

70 Paint your wood spirit in your desired color scheme.
Then finish with a polyurethane or acrylic spray sealer.

Tiki Topper

It seems that just about every culture has its own version of one of my favorite carving subjects, the Wood Spirit. In the Polynesian islands, it would be the tiki, which is a carving of a humanoid form that sometimes marks the boundaries of sacred sites. The delightful carved tiki face you'll be making uses leaves, geometric patterns, and expressive eyelids and mouth lines to give it emotional impact.

Since each specific feature of the tiki face is a simple shape—such as a rounded half-circle for the eyelids and a teardrop shade for the nose—it makes a wonderful project for the new carver as you learn about your wood, your tools, and your cutting strokes. For the advanced carver, it is a great subject for trying new ideas, techniques, and cutting styles. So whether this is your first carving or your hundredth, you will surely enjoy creating this cane topper.

Roughing Out the Shape

Materials

- Tiki Topper pattern (page 139)
- 1¼" x 1¼" x 4" (3.2 x 3.2 x 10cm) basswood block
- Bench knife
- Small round gouge
- Large round gouge
- V-gouge
- Straight chisel
- Small skew chisel
- Detail knife
- Pencil
- Graphite paper
- 220- and 320-grit sandpaper
- Rifflers (small metal files)
- Compass
- Old toothbrush
- Soft, lint-free cloth

1 Mark both the top and bottom of a basswood block with diagonal lines to find the center point. Next, using a compass, mark a circle off that center point that touches the outer edges of the block. At this point, to make this tiki face into a cane topper you should use these guidelines to drill a ⅜" (1cm) hole into the bottom of the block to prepare it for a dowel or other attaching method (see page 20). This is not shown in this step-by-step sequence. Also leave a little extra area of uncarved wood at the bottom of the block while carving to allow space for a leather or cord wrap later.

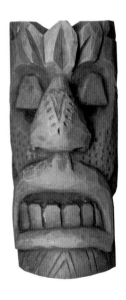

2 Begin this carving by rounding over the four sharp edges of your block with a bench knife or large chip carving knife. Note that I am using several safety methods at once while carving; I always use at least two out of three of the following when doing any three-dimensional carving: a thumb guard, a carving glove, or a thick terry cloth towel to hold the carving. As you work through this project, you will see that I have literally worn out my thumb guard beyond repair.

3 Work the sides until you bring the edges down to slightly larger than your compass circle on three sides. On the face side, allow extra wood. My face side is on the left in the photo. As you round over the sharp edges, work from the center of the block toward the top or bottom edge. This leaves a slight bulge at the centerline of the block. You will use that bulge point as the bottom edge of the nose.

4 Draw a pencil line around the rounded block at the bottom of the bulge area. Note as shown in the photo that you can grip the pencil and brace your hand with your small finger on the bottom of your block to use your hand just like a compass. This makes a fairly accurate line as you turn the block around the pencil.

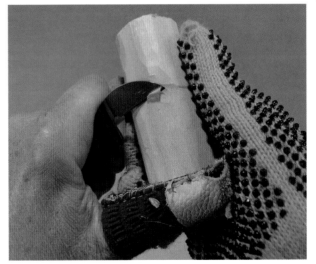

5 Using your bench knife, deepen the shelf of the nose—the bottom edge of the nose—by using a paring cut on the wood below the nose. The paring cut is made by pulling the knife toward you. It is the same as a pull cut.

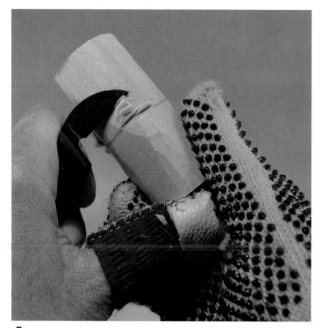

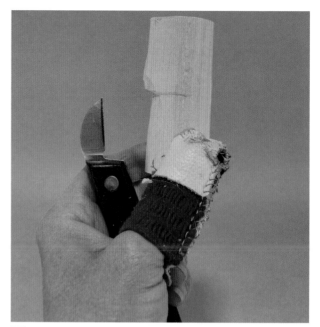

6 Make several paring cuts, working toward the bottom of the block. Turn the block over in your hand and work the paring cut into those previously made. This will lift the chips from under the nose.

7 Flatten the edge under the nose all the way to the bottom of the block.

Carving the Eyes and Nose

8 With a pencil, mark a line ½" (1.5cm) from the top of the block. Mark a vertical line from the top of the block through the center line of the nose. Mark the sides of the nose. Finally, make two half-circle arches just under the ½" (1.5cm) line for the eyebrow ridge.

9 With a bench knife or large chip carving knife, make a stop cut along the pencil line for the side of the nose. Hold the knife at a 90-degree angle to the wood and make a shallow cut. Repeat several times to slowly deepen the cut.

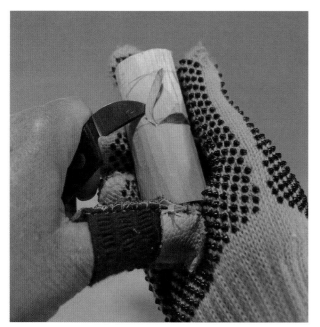

10 Lower the knife to about 45 degrees to the wood at the stop cut. Make a new cut about ⅛" (0.3cm) from the stop cut with the point of the knife at the stop cut. This will lift a triangle-shaped sliver of wood from the face.

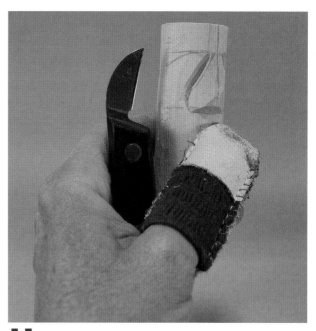

11 Repeat for the other side of the nose.

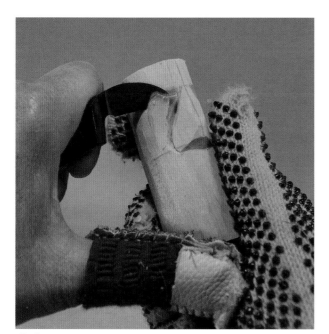

12 Using the bench knife or large chip carving knife and a paring cut, begin lowering the cheek area under the brow ridge line beside the nose. Roll the knife from shallow along the brow ridge to the depth of the side of the nose at the nose shelf.

13 Turn your block upside down and, using the paring cut, work back into the eye area to release the chips just made.

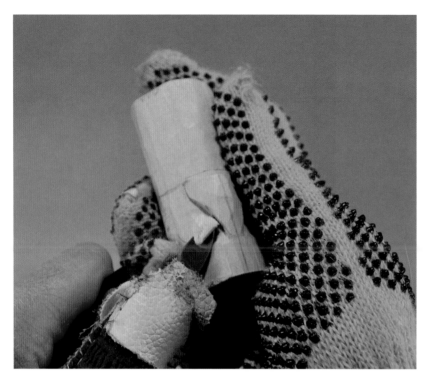

14 Repeat on the other side of the face. Or, alternatively, you can work each individual step and movement on both sides of the face at the same time. I often like to work this way. So here, for example, I will cut the stop cut along the side of the nose on both sides, then lower the eye area on both sides, then go on to the next step, working it on both sides. For me, this keeps the work fairly even.

15 To deepen the overhang of the eyebrow ridge, use a small ⅛" (0.3cm) to ³⁄₁₆" (0.5cm) round gouge along the eye area at the brow ridge pencil line. This cut is across the grain, whereas the previous paring cuts with the bench knife were worked with the grain. Cross-grain cuts can be slightly ragged along the edge, as shown in the photo. If your edge is excessively ragged or you have chip out—small triangles of lifted wood—you need to sharpen your gouge.

16 Work several gouge cuts in this area to blend it with the paring cuts.

Carving the Mouth and Brow

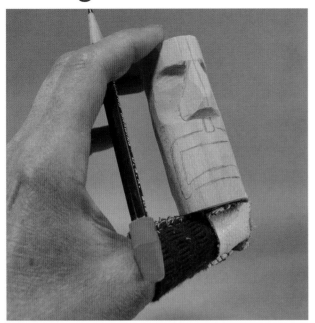

17 With the eyebrow ridges, eye and cheek areas, and nose established, it is time to mark a pencil line for the mouth and lip fold.

18 Using a large chip knife and a push stroke, lower the upper lip where it touches the nose shelf. Work both sides of the upper lip from the lip fold toward the outer edge of the mouth. A detail knife, which has a longer and narrower blade edge than a chip knife, works wonderfully for this step.

19 Use a small round gouge to create the lip fold. Using this gouge, cut up toward the nose shelf. Next, use your bench knife or chip knife to stop cut the gouge stroke, releasing the wood sliver.

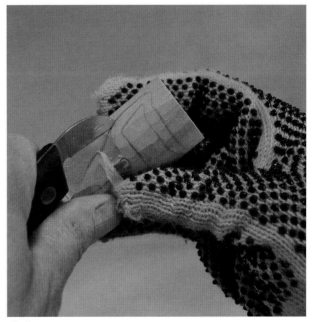

20 Stop cut along the outer edge of the mouth. Using a paring cut, lower the wood outside the mouth edge to make the mouth appear raised.

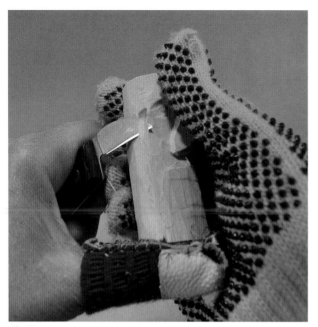

21 As you are lowering the wood outside the mouth edge, even the sides of the face to the depth of the wood along the sides of the mouth. Lower the wood below the mouth, referring to the original compass circle line on the bottom to keep this area as round as possible.

22 Repeat for the inside of the mouth. Cut a stop cut along the inside mouth line using your bench knife. Then use a paring cut to cut from the center of the mouth into the stop cut to lower the inside of the mouth area.

23 To begin creating the eye area, you first need to establish the nose bridge. Using a bench knife and the push stroke, taper the nose from one quarter of the nose length from the nose tip toward the intersection of the two eyebrow ridge half-circles.

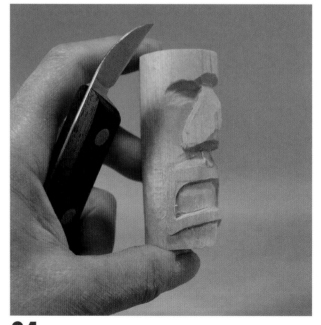

24 Drop the top point of the nose at the bridge to almost level with the eye areas.

Adding Facial Details

25 While you are working this area, also lower the forehead area, sloping it toward the top of the block, away from the brow ridge lines.

26 With a pencil, create an elongated half-circle in the eye area for the upper eyelid. Mark a small half-circle below this for the eye. Also mark where you want the tooth line in the mouth.

Eyelids are an easy way to create new and distinct faces. You can use one eyelid on the top or use two—one for the top and one for the bottom lid. You can slant the straight edge of the top lid to give your tiki emotions. If you draw a line from the top point of the nose bridge down toward the outer corner of the mouth, your tiki will look sleepy or lazy. Reverse that slant with the high side at the outer corner of the brow ridge down toward the nostrils, and your tiki becomes angry. Try changing the sizes of your eyelids. Use a small or narrow half-circle lid on the top and an elongated, large lid on the bottom to give him baggy eyes.

27 With your V-gouge, cut along the pencil line of the eyelid half-circle. This drops the wood just a small amount.

28 Use your bench knife to lower the wood in the wood surrounding the eyelid.

29 For tight corners, such as where the eyelid touches the side of the nose, you can use one corner of the cutting edge of your round gouge to tease out the excess wood.

30 Then follow this cutting stroke with a stop cut with your bench knife to lift the wood slivers.

31 Lower the wood in the cheek area with a push cut into the lower edge of the eyelid V-gouge trough.

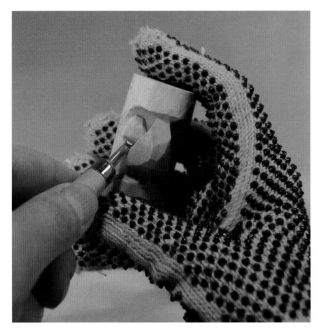

32 You can treat the actual eye with one of two methods. You can stop cut along the half-circle line with your bench knife, then shave the wood surrounding the eye, cutting into that stop cut. This will create a small, raised eye area. But I prefer the other method—to cut out the eye. Upend your small round gouge so that the cutting edge is sitting at a little less than 90 degrees from the wood. Push the gouge into the wood, cutting a deep, round trough.

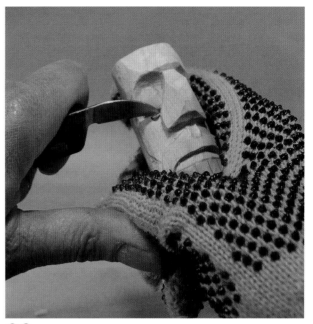

33 Then, with your bench knife, cut along the top edge of the round gouge cut at the eyelid line to free the small half-circle wood sliver. A cut-in round gouge eye like this is quick, easy, and very, very round. If you antique your carving later, the dark stain will fill the eyeholes, creating a dark eye look.

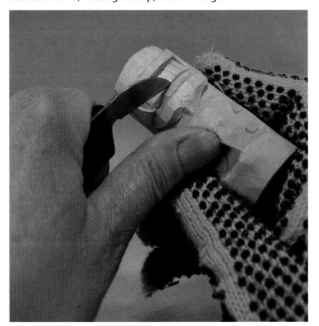

34 To create the row of bottom teeth, use a bench knife to make a stop cut along the top edge of the row. Continue this stop cut along the inside of the mouth at the bottom edge of the upper lip.

35 Using the small round gouge or bench knife, lower the wood level in the mouth between the top edge of the teeth and the lower edge of the upper lip.

Tikis have teeth—lots and lots of exaggerated teeth. They also commonly come with tongues that are sticking out. As with eyes, this is another area where you can be very creative in changing your tiki's face and expression.

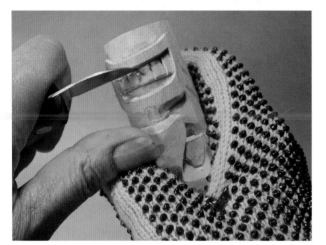

36 Using either the V-gouge or a stop cut made with the bench knife, cut a shallow V-trough line between each of the teeth. Make a very small stop cut at the corner of each tooth to cut a small triangle between the teeth.

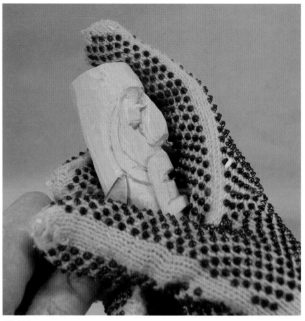

37 Mark two half-circles into the sides of the face, starting at the top edge of the eyebrow ridge and running to the side of the mouth. With a V-gouge, cut a trough along these lines. Use your bench knife to lower the wood on the side of these lines on the outside edge of the face.

38 Round over the raised edge of these half-circle decorations using the bench knife.

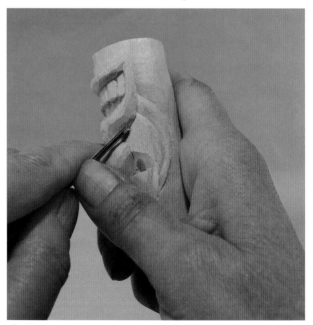

39 A very small 1⁄16" (0.2cm) V-gouge makes a narrow, shallow cut. Cut along each of the stop cuts in the carving to clean the lines of any remaining wood fibers and give all of the edges a neat, trimmed finish.

Detailing and Finishing

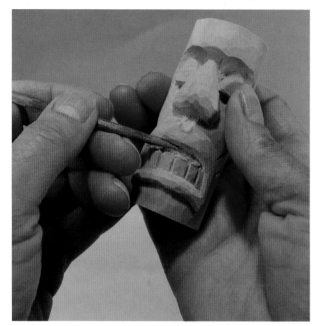

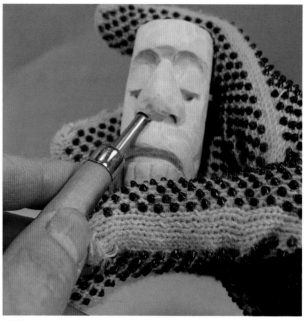

40 The main carving on the face is complete, so it is a good time to continue with a quick cleanup. I use 220-grit sandpaper, small rifflers (thin metal files), and foam core nail files to dress out the carvings. Foam core nail files can be cut with scissors to make small, stiff sanding boards for tight spaces. When the sanding is finished, use either an old toothbrush or stiff paintbrush to remove the sanding dust.

41 To create the nostrils, upend a small round gouge. Holding the gouge at a 90-degree angle under the nose shelf, cut a deep half-circle cut. Use your bench knife to slice along the top edge of this half-circle to remove the wood chip.

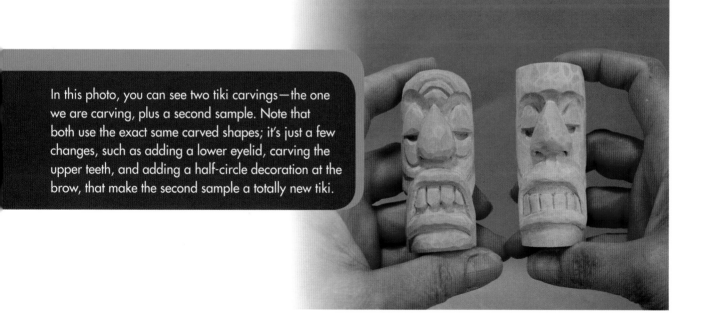

In this photo, you can see two tiki carvings—the one we are carving, plus a second sample. Note that both use the exact same carved shapes; it's just a few changes, such as adding a lower eyelid, carving the upper teeth, and adding a half-circle decoration at the brow, that make the second sample a totally new tiki.

42 Let's add more flair to this basic tiki by giving him a small crown. Begin by marking pencil lines for three leaves above the eyebrow ridge, centered over the nose bridge. Also mark a pencil line ¼" (0.5cm) from the top edge of the block.

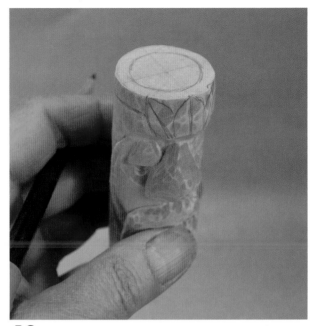

43 On the top of the block, mark a circle about ³⁄₁₆" (0.5cm) from the edge. This will be the inside guideline for the leaves and crown points.

44 Make sure that your large round gouge is nice and sharp. Starting at the marked guideline, roll the large round gouge across the top of the block, toward the center, to create a bowl shape. You are working across the grain.

45 My bowl developed a small area at the center that was not easy to reach with the round gouge rolled cutting stroke. To remove it easily, I first scored this area with my bench knife, cutting straight into the wood for about ¹⁄₁₆" (0.2cm). I cut multiple slices across this bulge, then turned the piece and cut again at a right angle to the first cuts. This created a tight crosshatching of straight cuts into the grain. When I returned to my large round gouge, this area cut easily, releasing small, rectangular chips.

46 Add a pencil line just above the outer edge of the eye decoration rings. The small crown will only appear in the front half of the chess piece; this line marks where to simply roll over the back of the head.

47 Roll the back of the head using a bench knife and push cuts. When working a large rounded-over area, make a layer of cuts over the area, then return and do a second and even third cutting until you have an even, smooth roll.

48 Using the bench knife, cut out small triangles between the leaf points. Again, since this is cutting into the end grain, take small, narrow slices to create the final V-cut instead of trying to work the cut in one step.

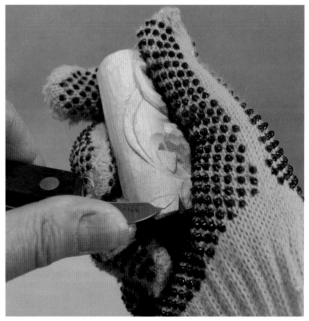

49 To add just a touch of decoration, make a chip cut in the crown point behind the leaves. Start by using the bench knife to make a stop cut into the wood along one side of the triangle.

50 Repeat this cut for the second side, then the third.

51 The third cut will lift a small triangle chip from the wood.

52 Separate each of the leaves with a stop cut using your bench knife.

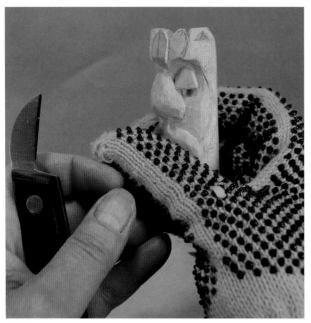

53 Lower the wood on the outer side of each leaf—the side farthest from the face. This will tuck the two side leaves under the center leaf.

54 Finally, cut a stop cut along the center vein line of each leaf. This completes the carving for the tiki face. At this point, do another cleanup session to dress out any loose fibers, rough cuts, and joint lines. Also do a light sanding over the uncarved back area of this cane topper.

Twistie Snake Topper

This particular design—a snake wrapped around a sassafras twistie stick—is a beginner's level project, but I think that even advanced carvers may discover a few fun tricks and tips here. We will work, step by step, through creating the round, establishing the snake, marking and cutting the twist, texturing the snake and bark, adding a frog on the top of the stick, and adding a real honeysuckle vine into the twist. Because we will be creating the pattern directly on the basswood, you can make this topper in any length. The cane will be lightly coated with a linseed oil and turpentine finish and then dry-mounted to your walking staff.

Materials

- 1½" x 1½" x 12" (3.8 x 3.8 x 30.5cm) basswood block
- Bench knife or large chip carving knife
- V-gouge
- ⅜" (1cm) round gouge
- ⅛" (0.3cm) round gouge
- U-gouge
- Several sizes of fine rifflers (metal files)
- 220-grit sandpaper
- 1" (2.5cm)–wide painter's tape or masking tape
- Pencil
- Old toothbrush
- Cardboard center from a roll of toilet paper
- Linseed oil
- Turpentine
- All thread rod
- Epoxy glue
- Walking stick staff, approx. 4' (122cm) to 5' (152cm) tall x 1¼" (3.2cm) diameter

Creating the Snake Body

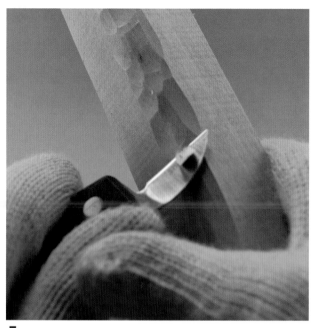

1 Use your bench knife and a push stroke to round over the edges of the basswood block. Work the cuts from the sharp corner toward the center of each flat face of the block.

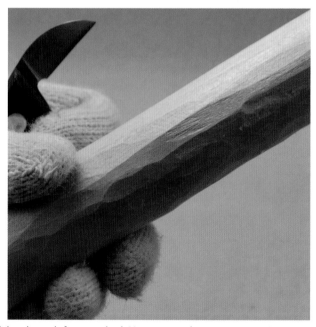

2 A well-rounded stick will have all of the original surface area cut. Note in this photo that no area of the block has been left unworked. No matter what you are carving, at some point during any carving you will want to ensure that you have actually carved all the wood. The milled surface of a basswood block has a very different texture than the cut areas. After you have added a finish, that difference will dramatically stand out, making the uncarved areas an eyesore.

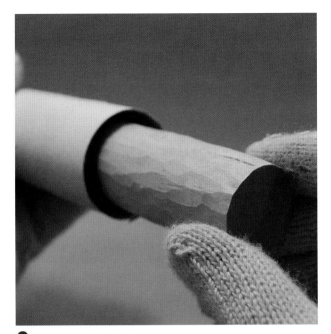

3 I like to double-check my round by comparing the basswood block to something that I know is a true circle or close to a true circle. For this project, that true circle is the inside of a cardboard tube from a toilet paper or paper towel roll. By sliding the wood inside the cardboard tube, I can check for flat surfaces or planes that need a little more work.

4 To easily create the path of the snake around the basswood block, we will use painter's tape. Mark a roll of painter's tape at ⅝" (1.5cm). For this cane, that will be the width of the snake's body. With your bench knife, cut a strip of tape long enough to wind around your wood.

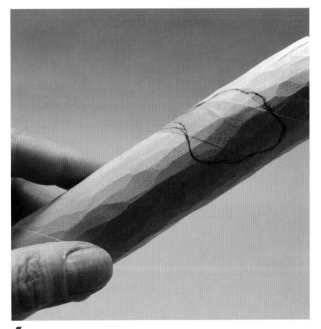

5 Secure one edge of the tape at the bottom of your stick, and roll the tape around the stick until you reach the top. My tape ran at about a 45-degree or smaller angle. Looking at the stick with the bottom edge of the tape facing me, I have four wraps, with the last wrap right at the top of the stick.

6 Using a pencil or marker, draw or trace the pattern for the snake head about 1" (2.5cm) down from the top of the stick, right on top of the painter's tape. See page 120 for more detail and the pattern.

The snake head pattern is simple to pencil-mark directly on your wood. Begin with an equilateral triangle twice the size of the snake's neck width. Make a pencil line at each corner of the triangle to slice off the sharp edges. Now add a small half-circle just in front of the center point on each side of the triangle for the eyes. That's it—you've done it!

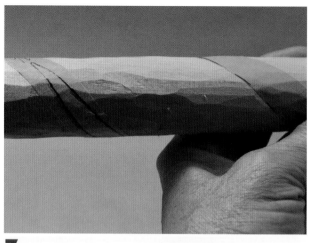

7 Mark two tapered lines for the tip of the tail of the snake on the tape. Begin the tail about 1" (2.5cm) above the bottom of the stick.

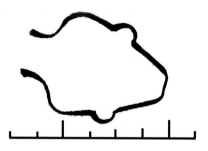

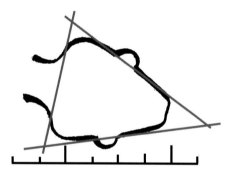

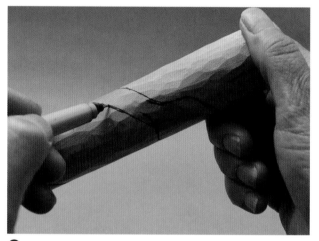

8 Using a pencil or marker, trace along the edges of the tape to mark on the wood the snake's body lines.

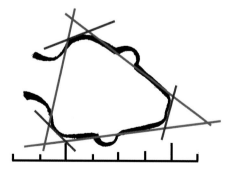

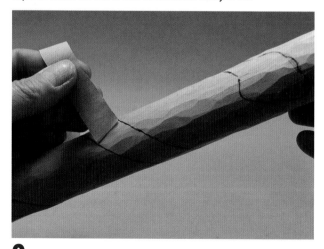

9 Remove the tape. You can rewrap painter's tape on the roll and reuse it later for your next snake walking stick or for securing paper patterns and graphite paper to other carvings.

10 Create a stop cut along the outer edge of the snake body lines, cutting on the drawn guidelines. First, holding the knife at a 90-degree angle to the wood, cut along the line. Next, slice into the first cut, moving from the background area toward the snake body.

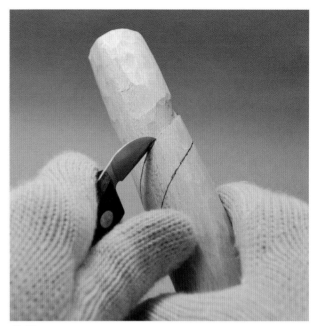

11 Start lowering the wood outside the snake body using stop cuts. I prefer to slowly drop the background wood in a stop cut area in thin layers or slivers at a time. As you work, you can make the first cut slightly shallow and then make the second background sliver into that cut. Then return to the snake body line and make a new, slightly deeper first cut. Again, work the second background sliver. This will slowly drop the background level of the wood, giving you more control over your depth of work.

12 Continue working the two strokes of the stop cut along both sides of the snake body. The stop cuts are worked about ⅜" (1cm) to ½" (1.5cm) away from the body lines of the snake. This leaves the center area of the space between the snake twists high (or proud). Those areas will later become the sassafras twists.

13 Work the stop cut around the snake's head. Notice that the snake's body has been completely freed from the background wood by dropping the background areas all around it.

A twisted sassafras stick is caused by honeysuckle vine curling around the trunk when the tree is still a year-old or two-year-old sapling. As the tree grows, so does the vine, reaching higher into the tree and thickening in width. Over the years, the vine begins to strangle the sassafras trunk, forcing the tree to grow around the embedded vine. You can see in the photo that this process affects both plants. The sample is a wild cherry sapling that is already developing a deep spiral scar. The honeysuckle develops a flattened side where it is in direct contact with the sapling. Sassafras, black cherry, dogwood, and even young black walnut are common twistie sticks, as they share the same environment as honeysuckle: abandoned roadsides and old fence rows.

The second photo shown here is a very old piece of wild grape vine, approximately 1½" (3.8cm) thick. The vine had been dead for several years because of tree trimming by the power company, so it was ready to harvest. You can see the power and strength of the twist in this grapevine, as it literally brought down the farm fence on which it grew.

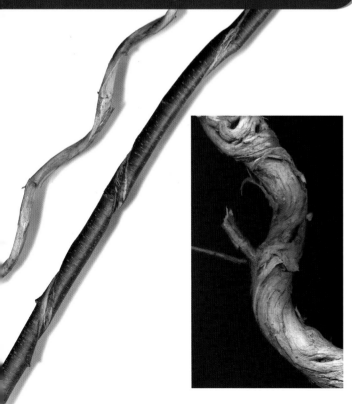

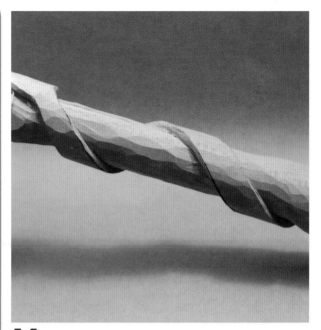

14 Work the stop cuts along the entire snake body until you are about ¼" (0.5cm) deep at the marked guidelines.

Creating the Twist

15 Using a marker or pencil, draw a line in the center of the area between the snake's body twists. This will be the path of the top edge of the twisted stick curls. On my cane, I had one area between the snake body curls that allowed for two twists. Draw a second guideline ¼" (0.5cm) below the first. This ¼" (0.5cm) area, between the two guidelines, will become the honeysuckle vine area on the twist.

16 Using your bench knife, work a stop cut along the top twistie guideline, in the background wood area. (In this photo, the cane is being held upside down.)

17 The second stroke of the stop cut lowers the background area at the top edge of the twist. (The cane is still being held upside down.)

18 Everything between the snake's body twists is sassafras wood. So the stop cuts in the previous steps taper that wood area into a cone shape that points down and into the top edge of the twist below it. To emphasize the taper of the twist, you can also use your large or small round gouge instead of the bench knife for the second stroke of the stop cut.

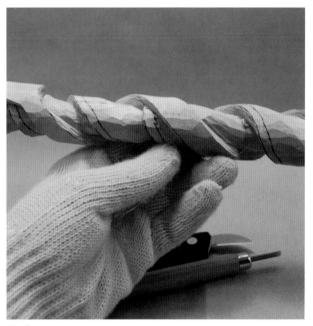

19 Here is the final result at this stage.

20 Using the bench knife, round over the top edge of the twistie curls, rolling the edge over to reach the second guideline mark.

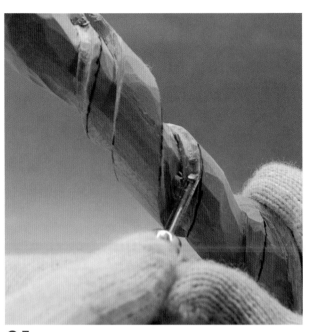

21 The honeysuckle will sit down and inside the sassafras wood. Create a half-circle trough using your small round gouge along the rounded-over top edge of the twist.

22 Cut this trough several times, slowly lowering it into the wood. In the photo, you can see the depth of the round gouge cuts in the second, right-hand twist.

23 With your bench knife, return to tapering the bottom section of each twist. Smooth each area of twist so that the taper moves evenly from thick at the top edge of the twist to thin at the bottom.

24 As you work the tapering, begin undercutting the bottom edge of each twist. This is done by angling the first stroke of the stop cut behind the inside edge of the top of the next twist. When you make the second stroke, it will pop out a small V-shaped chip, leaving a narrow cut behind the twist's inside edge.

25 Begin shaping the snake's body, head, and tail, using your bench knife to roll over the sides.

26 When the body has been shaped, the rough-out stage of this cane carving is complete. At this point you have established the curve and shape of the snake and the curve, tapering, and shape of the sassafras twist.

27 After the rough-out stage is done, I like to do a general smoothing of any project. This is done by recutting all of the areas you have worked with your bench knife. Drop the angle of the knife blade low to the wood, with the blunt or back side of the blade just five or six sheets of paper high off the wood. Lightly glide the knife across the wood, taking very small, shallow strokes. This image shows the cane's surface before the shaving step.

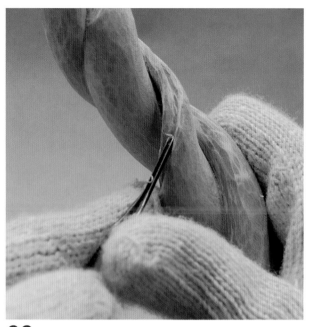

28 This image shows the shaving step completed. You can see the very fine, small cuts that smooth out the shape of the cane.

29 Very small, tight-arced round gouges are called veining tools. This tiny round gouge makes straight-walled, round-bottomed troughs, which are perfect for deepening the honeysuckle stem area.

30 Tear off a small square of 220-grit sandpaper and roll it tightly into a tube. Use the tube to sand the honeysuckle trough area along the top of each sassafras twist.

Working the Snake Head and Sassafras Texture

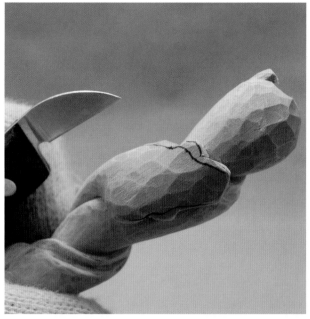

31 It's time to shape the snake's head. To begin this area, I re-marked the outline and eye placement of the snake with permanent marker. Since we will carve this area, any permanent marker marks will quickly be worked away.

32 Cut along the outer edges to reduce any excess wood from the head. Cut along the edge of the eye area with a stop cut to lower the eye slightly on the head.

33 Round over the eye area using a bench knife.

34 Make a small slice in the head at the outer corners of the eye to emphasize the eye and to create the impression of the jaw and cheek.

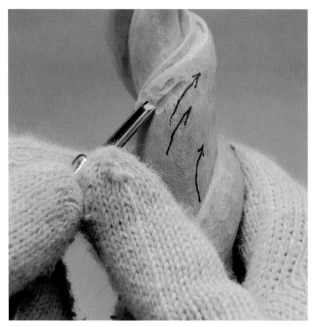

35 Texturing the sassafras bark is done with both the veining tool and a small round gouge. Cut small, shallow, tear-shaped gouge strokes in the bark area using the small round gouge first. I have marked cutting direction guidelines on the wood with marker.

36 Note in the photo that I am making the bark twist by angling my strokes with the curve of that twist area. Do a few veining tool cuts as well to add smaller texture strokes.

37 With the bench knife, make a few stop cuts along the top edge of the bark in the twist areas. These stop cuts make the bark appear cracked or split, which is a natural occurrence for any sassafras stick.

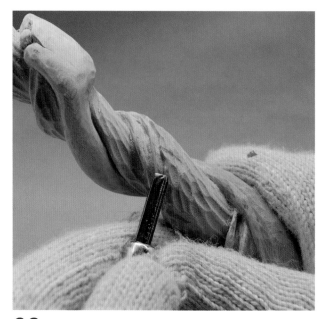

38 Bark lies on top of the wood of a stick. To emphasize that the bark and the wood are two different areas or elements, use your V-gouge to cut a small, thin trough where these two areas meet. You can also use your bench knife to make a few shallow undercuts into the bark to make it appear as if the bark is slightly peeling.

Adding Snake Scales

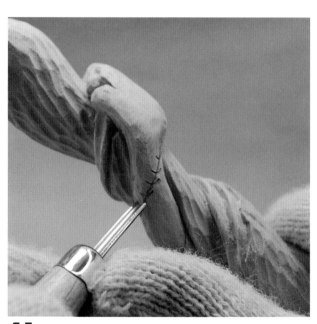

39 Do a little more sanding. These cleaning steps are technically called dressing out the wood and are used to catch little imperfections while you have them in your sights.

40 There are many, many ways to work the scaling of the body of a snake, lizard, or dragon. What I am using here is the most simple and foolproof method that I know. In working my snake, I lost just two scales—two that popped out during cutting—and my solution to those two was to simply ignore them. Mistakes happen, and sometimes trying to fix a mistake just makes it worse. Begin by marking parallel lines along the snake body lightly with pencil. Also take a moment a refresh the cutting edge of your small round gouge.

41 Upend your round gouge, holding it at a 90-degree angle to the wood so that the cutting edge is going straight into the wood. Gently push the gouge into the wood to cut a half-circle profile cut. Lift the gouge straight out of the wood. This is a simple push-and-lift stroke.

42 Work several upended small round gouge profile cuts along the guidelines to set the spacing of the rows. Then work off of that center cut to create the other profile cuts in the row. This style of scale creation will leave a very light, gentle impression of scales along the body. They will become more outstanding when you add the linseed oil finish later.

43 Some of the profile cuts made with my small round gouge were slightly lifted from the snake's body. To fix them, I rubbed the wooden handle of my gouge over the snake, moving from the head toward the tail. This light pressure sets the scales back against the wood. This process is called healing. Healing can be done at any time in a carving. For example, if you make a stop cut that is slightly too deep, turn your bench knife upside down after the second stroke is complete and place the blunt side against the deep cut. Use a medium pressure and pull the blunt side down the cut to heal it back together. Work carefully—in this example, that cutting edge is now facing toward your hand.

44 At this point, the work on the snake is complete and the sassafras carving is complete, except for adding the honeysuckle vine into the trough. This is a great stopping point if you are ready to take a break.

45 To do a little more cleanup, use sandpaper, rifflers, and your bench knife to dress out your cane.

Adding the Frog Topper and Honeysuckle Vine

46 To finish out the top of the cane and add some fun interest, we are going to add a small frog clutching the top of the stick, just out of reach of the snake's head. Freehand the frog or follow the pattern on page 141.

47 First, stop cut the frog using the bench knife along the outer edges of the frog's body. This separates him from the top area of the stick. Lower the cane top about ⅛" (0.3cm) at the frog's face and taper it down to ¼" (0.5cm) at the frog's rump.

48 Taper the stick twist area of the top to gradually flare.

49 Undercut the stick area into the top twist. This deepens the wood around the frog, making the frog appear to stand higher off the cane.

50 Shape the frog body, legs, and eyes using your bench knife to round over each area. With 220-grit sandpaper and rifflers, smooth out the frog.

51 You can harvest fresh honeysuckle vine to use on your sassafras twist cane. Select second-year growth or older; it will have a brownish tone to the paperlike bark. Green-tone bark is first-year growth and often is not strong enough to dry well. Roll the vine into a loose circle and hang in a dry, dark space for about three weeks. This is long enough for the vine to lose most of its sap and moisture but still remain pliable enough for curling. Strip the paper bark layer from the vine before you add it to your walking stick. Honeysuckle loses its bark easily. If you leave the bark on the vine, only the bark layer will be attached during the gluing. When the bark is shed, you will lose the vine around your cane. You can also purchase predried, prestripped honeysuckle vine, seagrass, raffia, and even paper rope from most basket weaving supply stores to use with your canes.

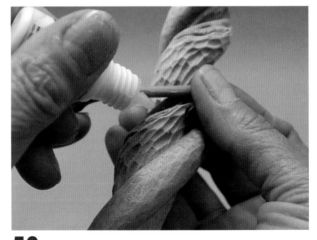

52 Soak your vine in warm (not hot) water for about 10 minutes. Lightly blot on a dry towel to remove the excess water from the outer surface. Check the thickness of your vine—the thinner part of the vine should be at the top of your stick, with the thicker, older growth at the bottom.

53 Using super glue, place several drops into the vine trough on your carving, then place the vine into the trough. Hold in place for about 30 seconds. Work just 1" (2.5cm) to 2" (5cm) at a time, slowly rolling the vine around the cane.

Finishing

54 Start cleaning with a hard scrubbing using an old toothbrush that can reach into the deep undercuts. Follow with a quick wash at the sink to remove any dirt and hand oils, using a small amount of dishwashing soap, warm water, and a small scrubbing brush. Rinse well, but do not oversaturate or soak the carving in the water. Blot the carving and allow to dry for about an hour.

55 To create the finishing mixture, mix one part linseed oil with one part turpentine. Stir well, but don't create bubbles. Brush one generous coat of the mix on all areas of the cane except the very bottom edge. Allow the oil mix to sit on the wood for ten minutes. Wipe briskly with a dry cloth to remove the excess oil. Repeat once more. This oil mix replaces the natural oils of the carving wood and soaks deeply into the wood fibers. After the oil finish has set for several days, you can return and apply whatever finish you personally prefer, such as polyurethane or paste wax.

56 My cane stick—a two- to three-year-old black walnut branch—was still green. So I decided to dry-set this stick, and not do the final glue-up until several months later. I drilled a ⅜" (1cm) hole into both the cane topper and the black walnut stick. For my dry set, I used a ⅜" (1cm) hardwood dowel, which will be replaced with ⅜" (1cm) threaded pipe for the final gluing. My dowel holes go as deeply as possible into both parts of the cane to give as long a section as possible for the jointing pipe.

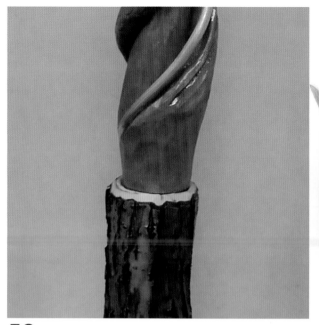

57 To hide the joint line between the cane topper and the stick, I have used my bench knife and small round gouge to cut a ¼" (0.5cm) deep well inside of the top of the black walnut stick. The outer ³/₁₆" (0.5cm) of the stick is left uncarved to create a lip area.

58 When the cane topper is put into place on its stick, the joint line between the two parts is hidden by the well area in the top of the stick.

59 In a couple of months, after the black walnut is well dried, I will set the cane using two-part epoxy and ³/₈" (1cm) threaded pipe.

Bonus Projects

Now that you have practiced with detailed step-by-step tutorials for several different kinds of cane toppers, here are a few fun mushroom carving projects for you to take a stab at. You'll be able to apply everything you've learned so far.

Little Reader Mushroom

Basic Materials

- 2½" x 2½" x 5" (6.5 x 6.5 x 12.5cm) basswood block for stem
- 3½" x 3½" x 2" (9 x 9 x 5cm) basswood block for cap
- 16-gauge copper wire for glasses
- Pattern on page 140

This carving uses a short, wide nose and extra-large mustache to make the face unique. Note in the finished sample that the mustache is larger in length than the facial features. Exaggerated mustaches and beards are a common feature of wood spirit faces.

The eyebrow overhang for this face is cut in a curve, arching at the center toward the forehead. The bottom line of the upper eyelid is curved, with the arch pointing down. This double arch—eyebrow and upper eyelid—gives the mushroom face a sleepy or lazy expression.

To emphasize the lazy look of this expression, several V-gouge wrinkles are cut below the lower eyelid in the cheek area. Start the wrinkle along the side of the nose and cut toward the outer edge of the face in a half-moon semicircle.

Because the tip of the nose is extra wide, a V-shaped wedge is cut along the bottom side of the nose to separate the bottom edge of the nostril from the ball tip of the nose. The cap is shaped to allow a portion of the underside of the cap to show. Large, 16-gauge copper wire glasses are the final touch to this face.

Large Cap Mushroom

Basic Materials

- 2" x 2" x 6" (5 x 5 x 15cm) basswood block for stem
- 4" x 4" x 2½" (10 x 10 x 6.5cm) basswood block for cap
- Pattern on page 142

Keep all of your scrap wood chips for this mushroom spirit! After the carving is complete, those chips are used to add the ragged feathers to the cap. This mushroom spirit face is identical to the GI Joe Mushroom (see page 63). To give him a unique personality, the eyes have been carved to be twice the size of the GI Joe Mushroom's, and a sharply pointed edging of extra fiber was worked along the base. The inner cap is worked as part of the facial piece and becomes the insert area that is set into the opening in the base of the large cap.

To add texture to the face, three rows of cheek wrinkles were cut using the V-gouge below the eye. A light carving with a small round gouge created the ribbed texturing in the face and back of the stem.

After the carving is complete, use carpenter's glue to set the cap onto the stem. Search through your pile of carving chip scraps. Select the thickest pieces. Using carpenter's glue, adhere two to three staggered rows of feathering to the bottom half of the top portion of the cap. Allow the glue to dry overnight, then give the cap a light sanding using 320-grit sandpaper. A primer coat, acrylic craft paints, and several coats of spray sealer will strengthen the feather chips.

Little Gentleman Mushroom

Basic Materials

- 2" x 2" x 4" (5 x 5 x 10cm) basswood block
- 16-gauge copper wire
- 1¼" (3.2cm) of 2mm copper chain
- Pattern on page 141

This carving is created using one block of wood. The mushroom cap is larger than the face area of the wood spirit and curves from one side on his face toward the opposite side. The forehead and brow ridge areas of the face are not worked, as the cap sits just above the upper eyelids. A copper wire monocle hooked to an eyelet with a short length of chain gives a touch of Old World charm to this quick little carving.

Chapter 7: Patterns

In this chapter, you will find so many great carving patterns for cane toppers that you probably won't know where to start. That's okay—you have the time to carve as many of your favorites as you want. In fact, you'll find that a surprising number of diverse carving patterns can be adapted to the round, skinny shape of a cane topper, so you certainly aren't limited to the projects and patterns given in this book. If you're really stumped about where to start, try deciding who you'd like to make a cane or walking stick for, and then select a pattern to suit his or her personality.

Project Patterns

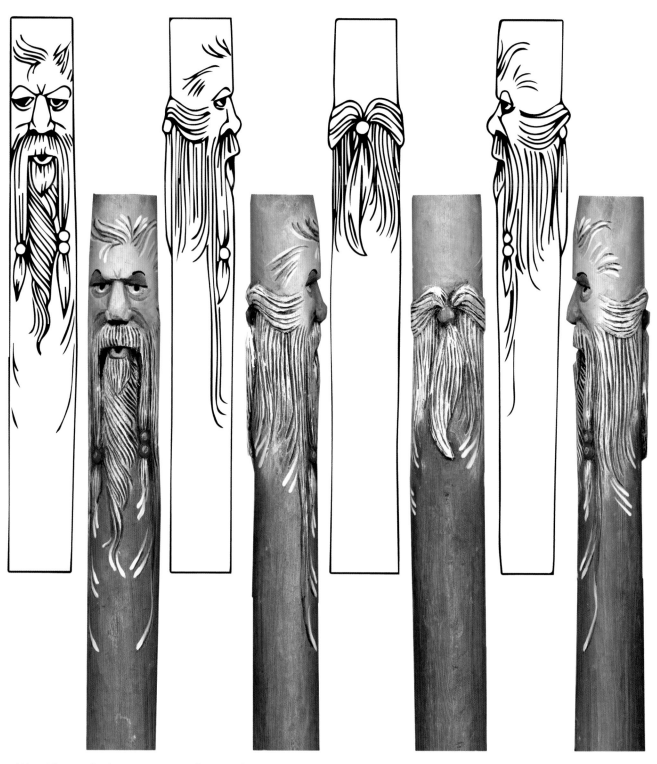

Wood Spirit - Scale pattern 125% for actual size

© Lora S. Irish

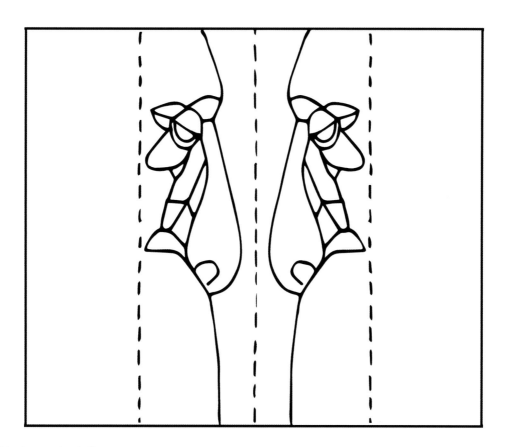

GI Joe Mushroom basic face

Tiki

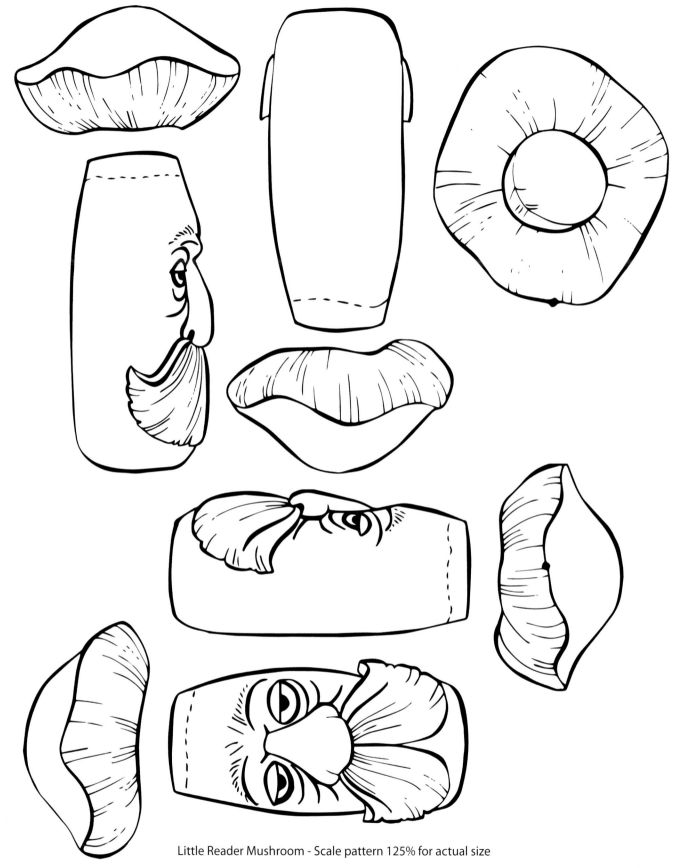

Little Reader Mushroom - Scale pattern 125% for actual size

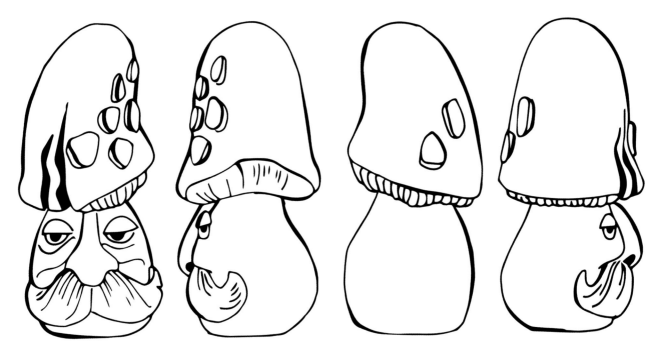

Little Gentleman Mushroom - Scale pattern 125% for actual size

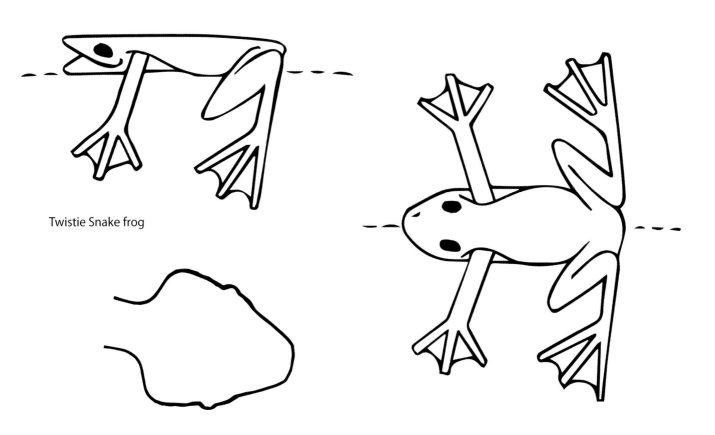

Twistie Snake frog

Twistie Snake snake head

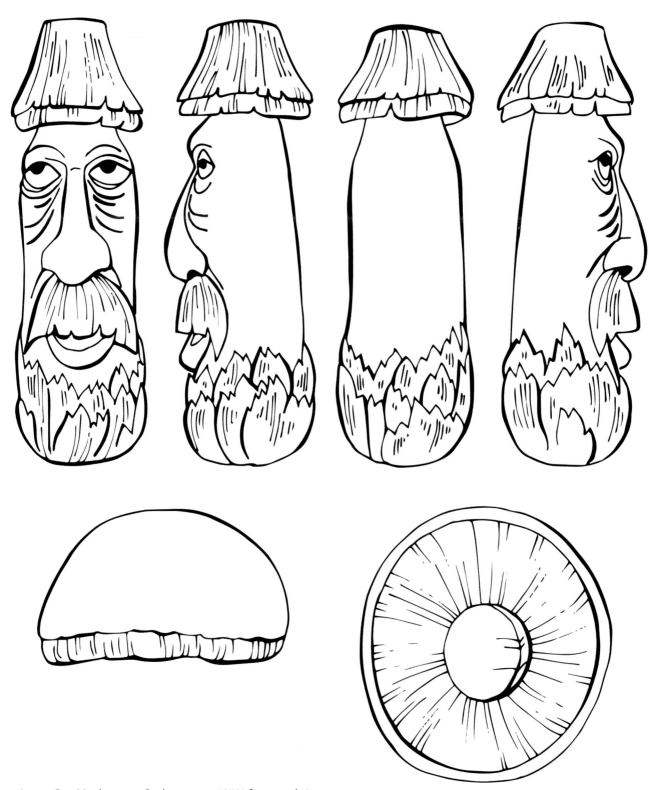

Large Cap Mushroom - Scale pattern 125% for actual size

Additional Patterns

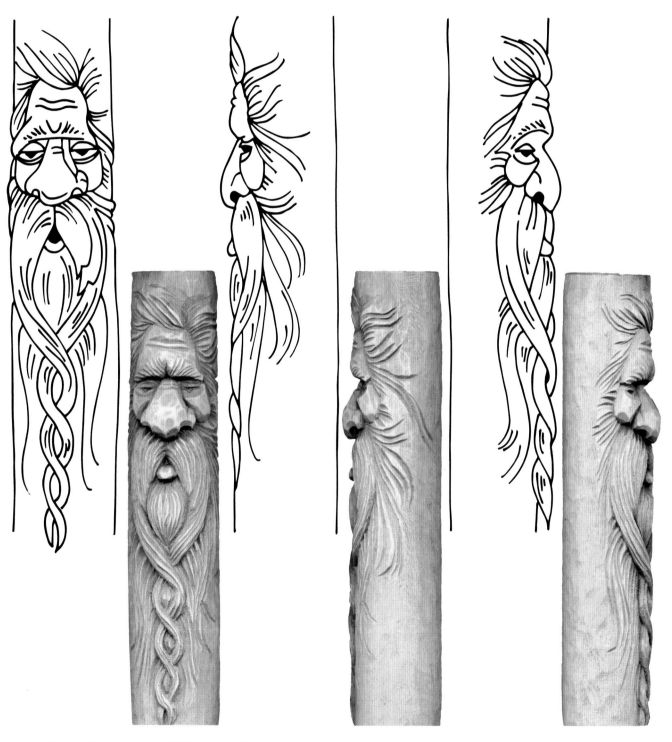

Twist Beard - Scale pattern 125% for actual size

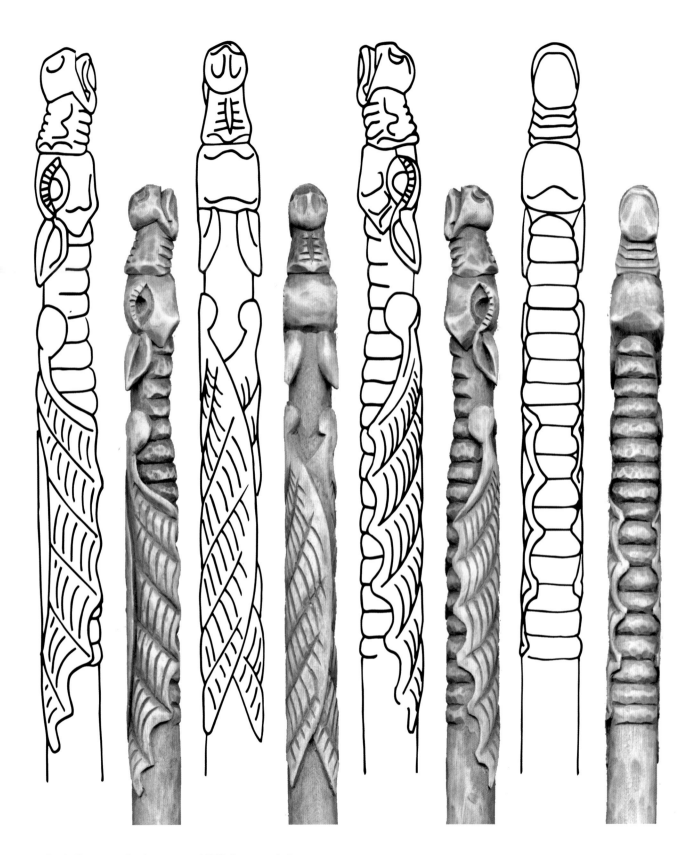

Basic Dragon - Scale pattern 125% for actual size

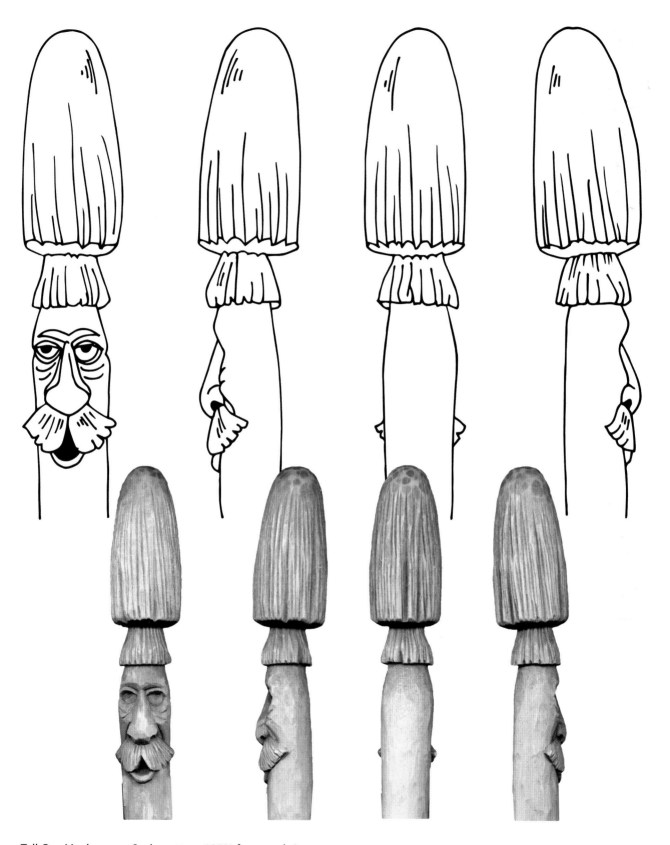

Tall Cap Mushroom - Scale pattern 125% for actual size

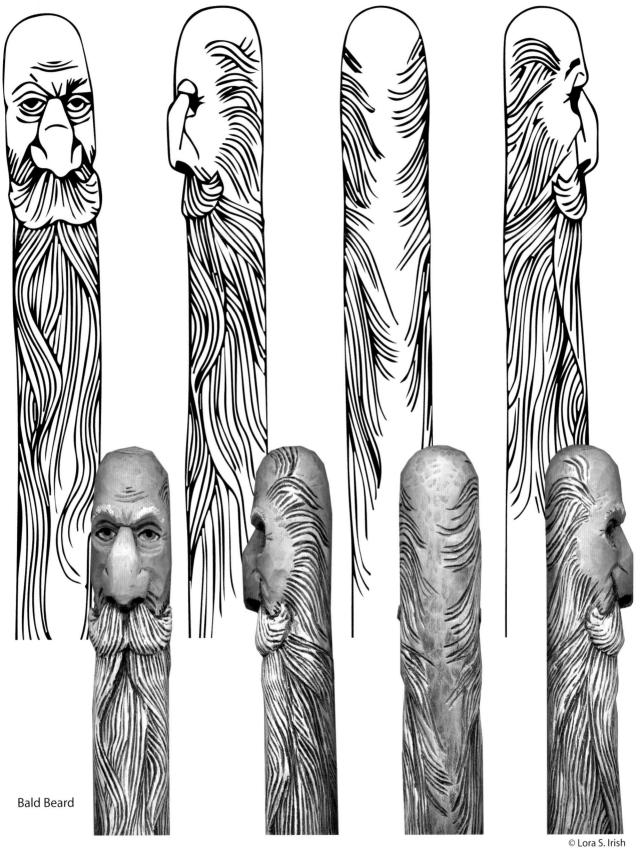

Bald Beard

© Lora S. Irish

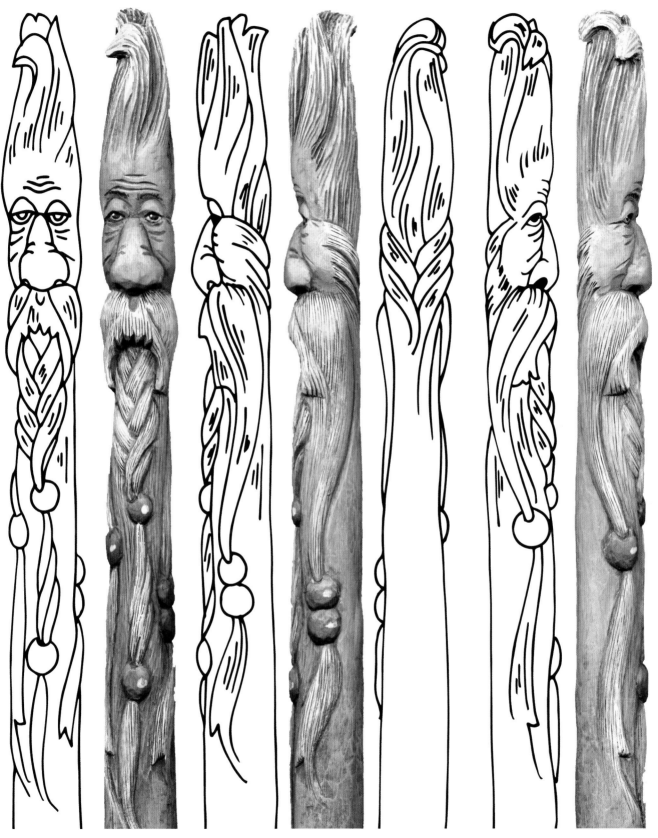

Blue Beads

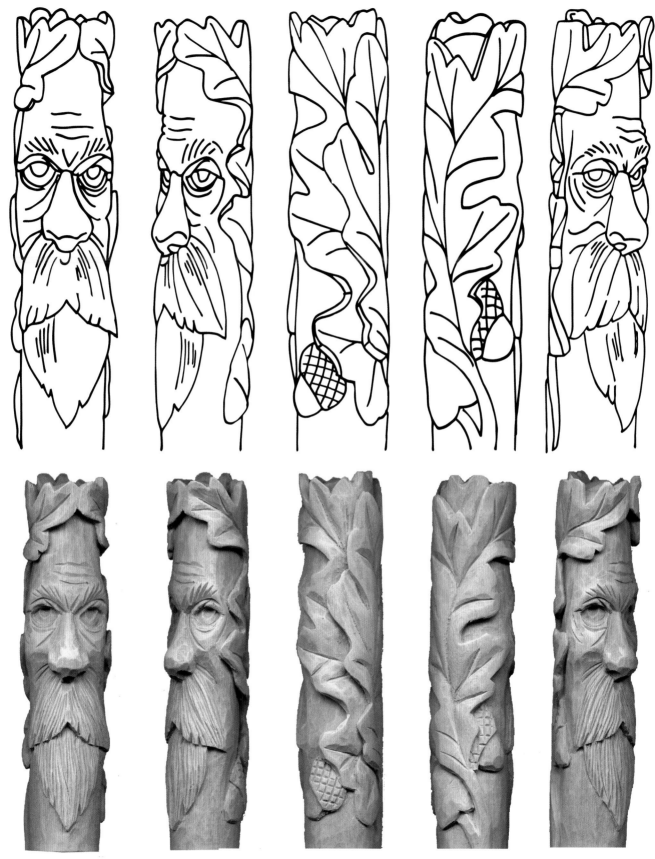

Oak Spirit - Scale pattern 125% for actual size

© Lora S. Irish

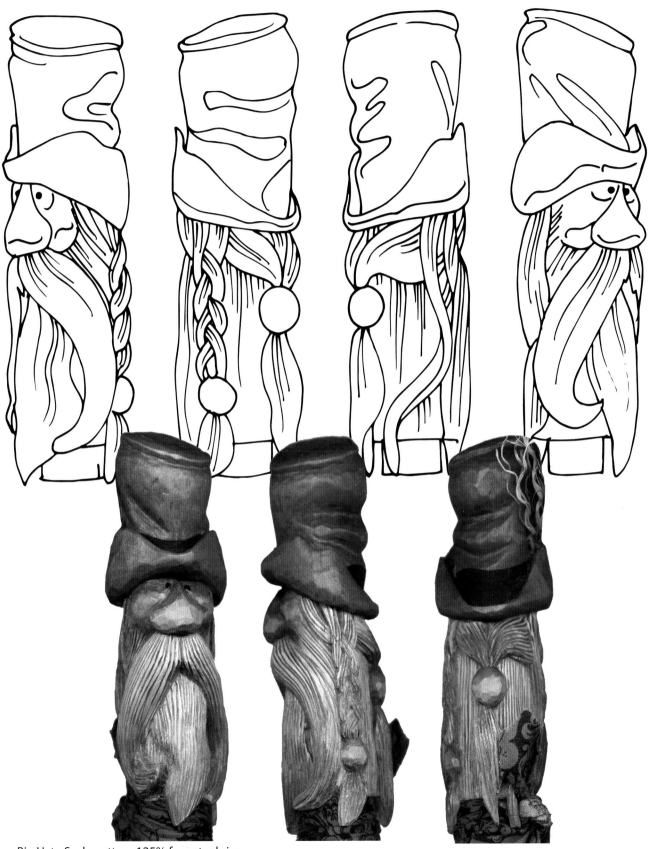

Big Hat - Scale pattern 125% for actual size

© Lora S. Irish

Basic Wood Spirit -
Scale pattern 125%
for actual size

© Lora S. Irish

Cane Shapes - Scale pattern 200% for actual size

© Lora S. Irish

Additional Patterns **151**

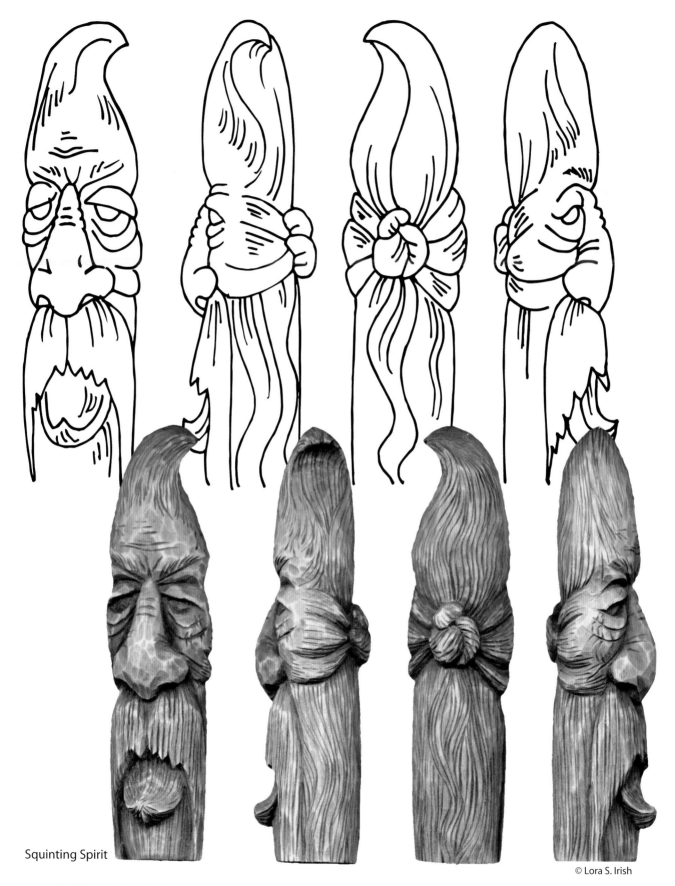

Squinting Spirit

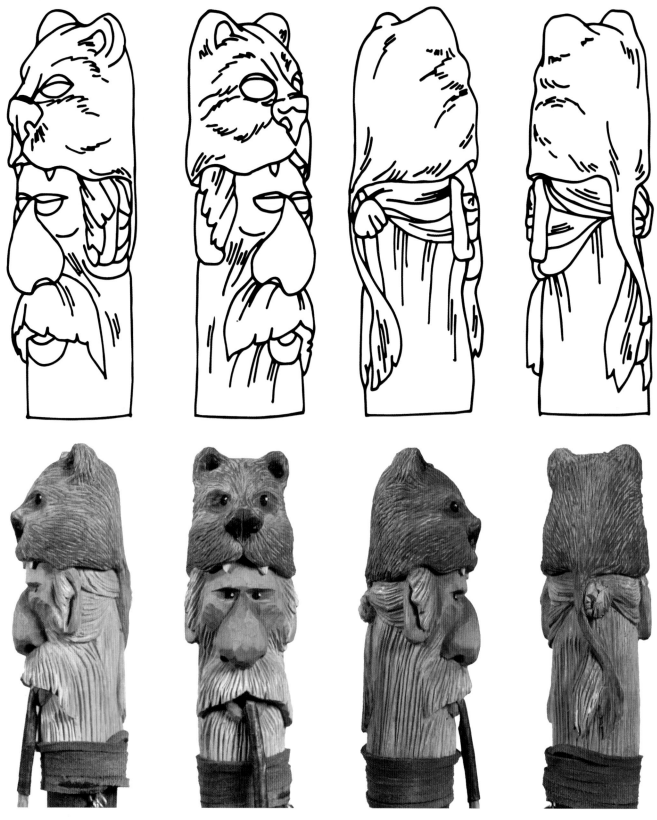

Hunter - Scale pattern 125% for actual size

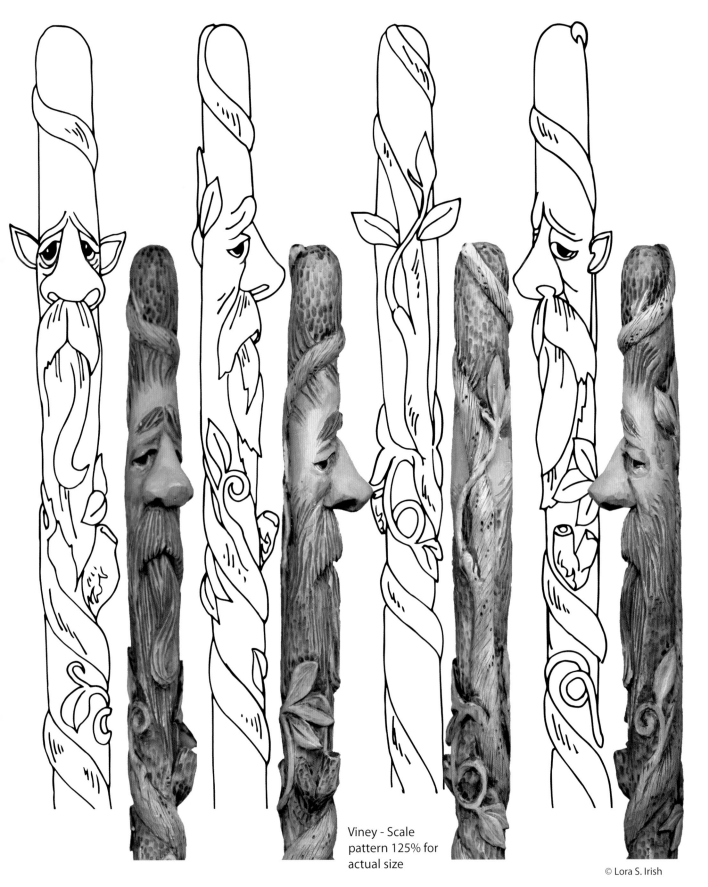

Viney - Scale
pattern 125% for
actual size

© Lora S. Irish

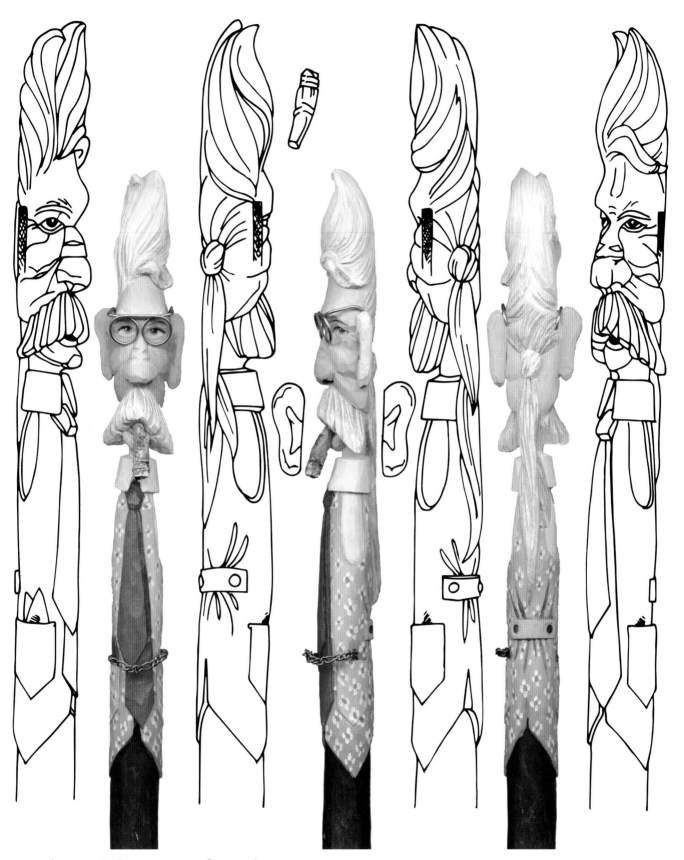

Mark Twain - Scale pattern 125% for actual size

Braided Beard

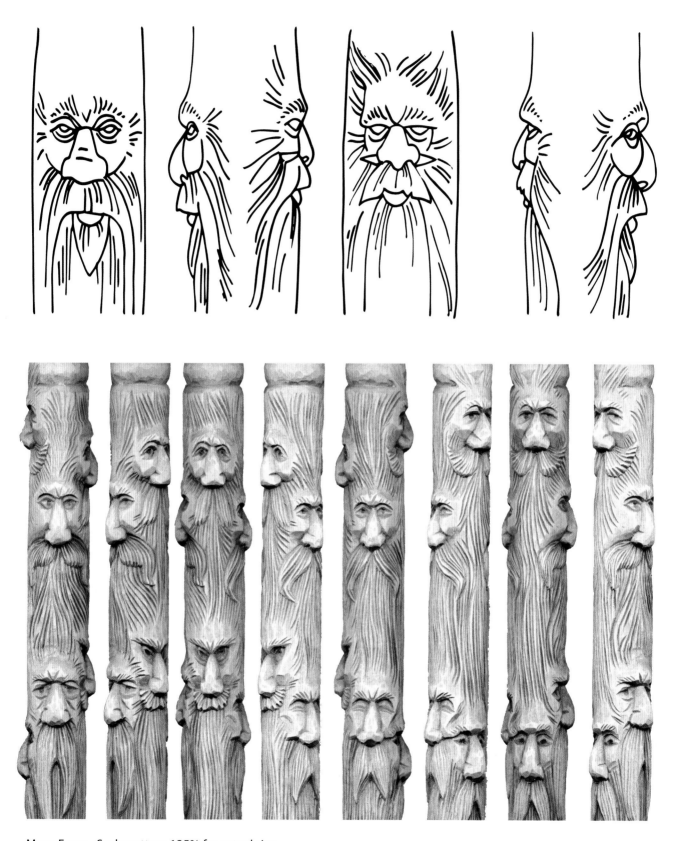

Many Faces - Scale pattern 125% for actual size

© Lora S. Irish

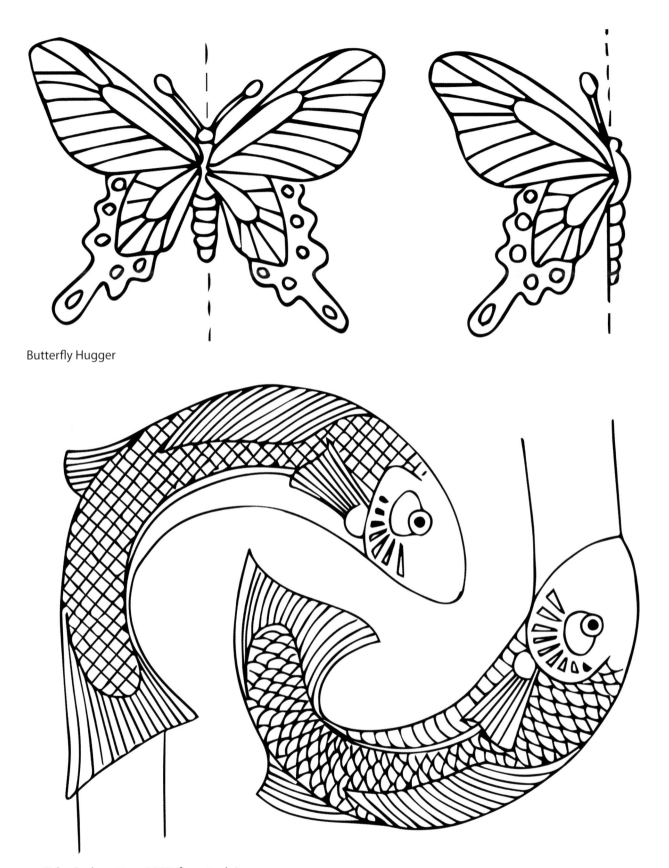

Butterfly Hugger

Fish - Scale pattern 125% for actual size

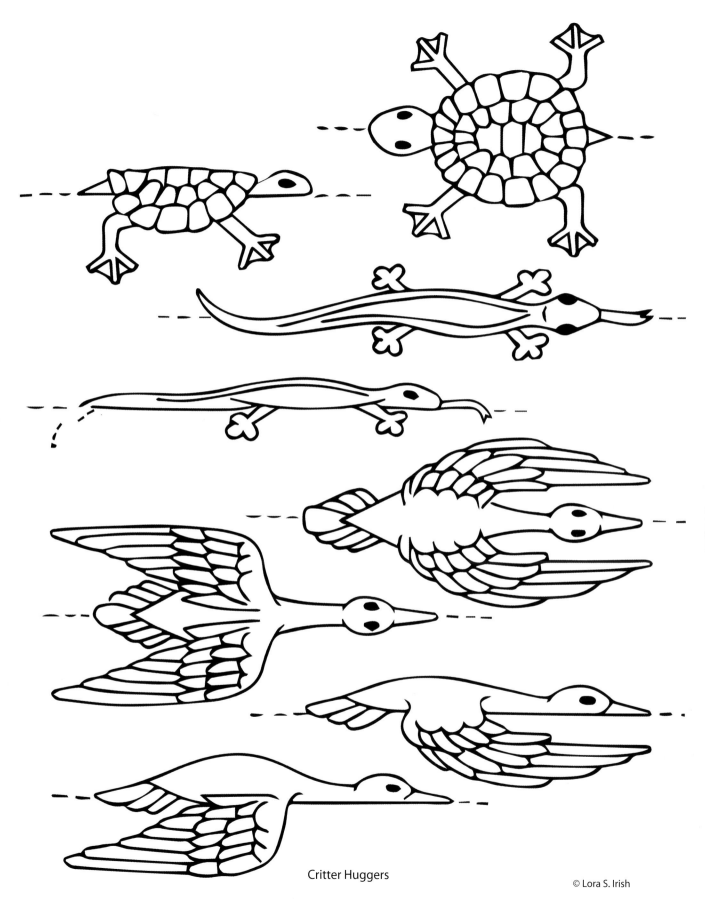

Critter Huggers

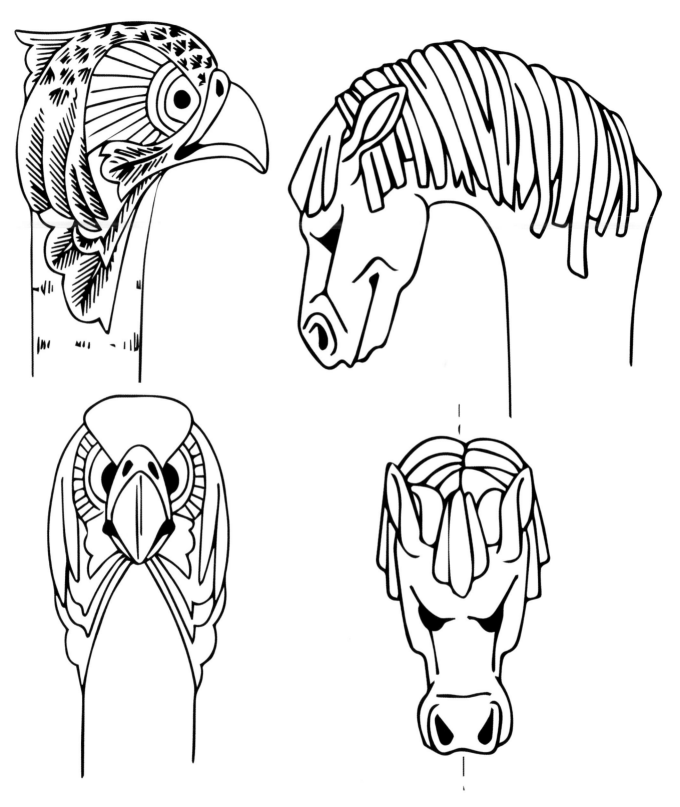

Fierce Eagle - Scale pattern 125% for actual size

Horse

Songbird - Scale pattern 125% for actual size

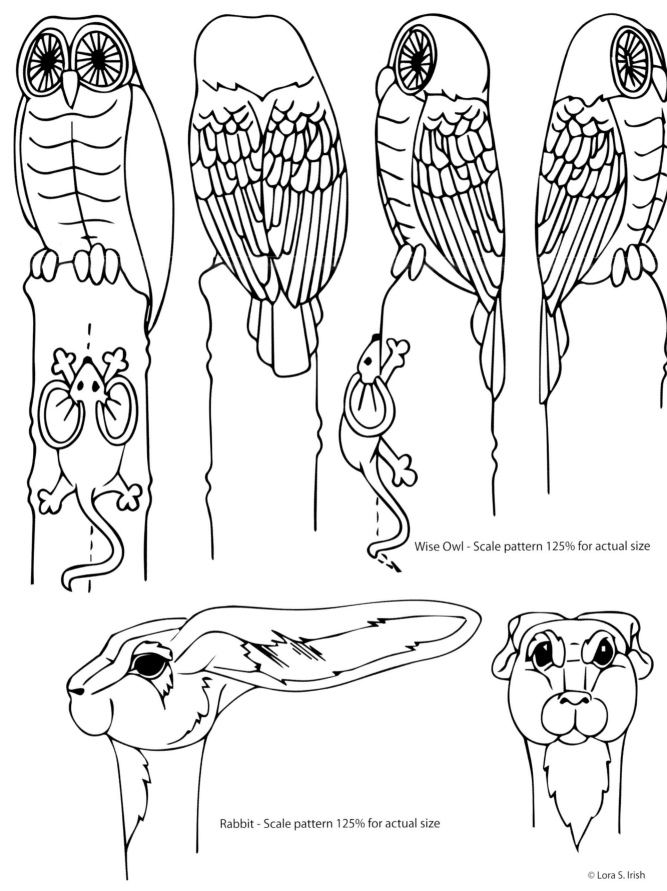

Wise Owl - Scale pattern 125% for actual size

Rabbit - Scale pattern 125% for actual size

© Lora S. Irish

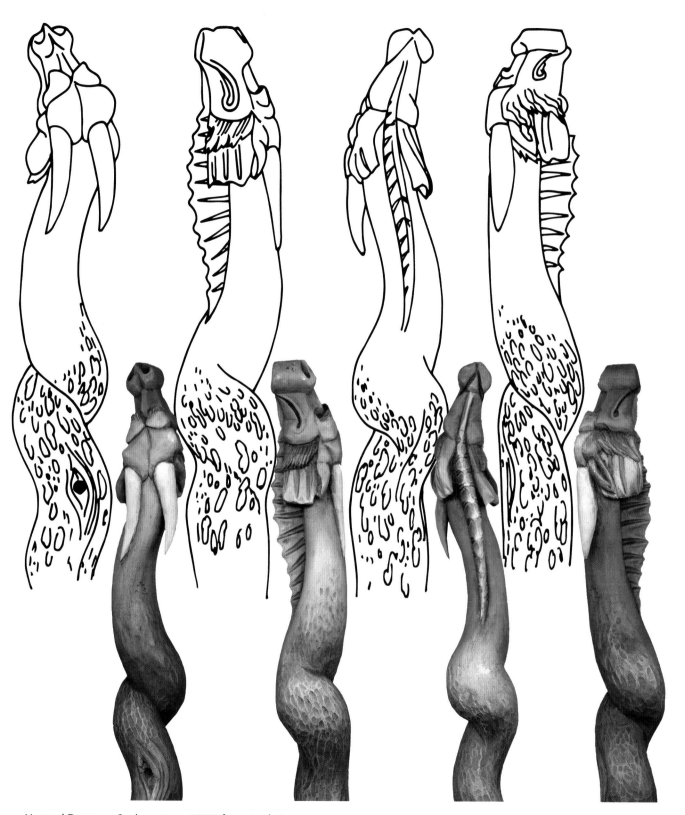

Horned Dragon - Scale pattern 125% for actual size

Additional Patterns **163**

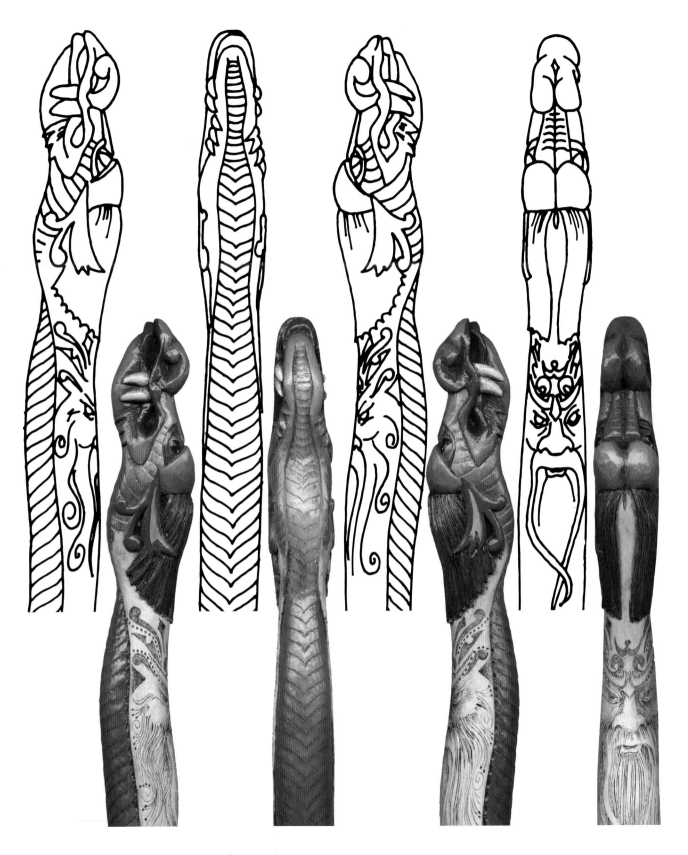

Vibrant Dragon - Scale pattern 125% for actual size

© Lora S. Irish

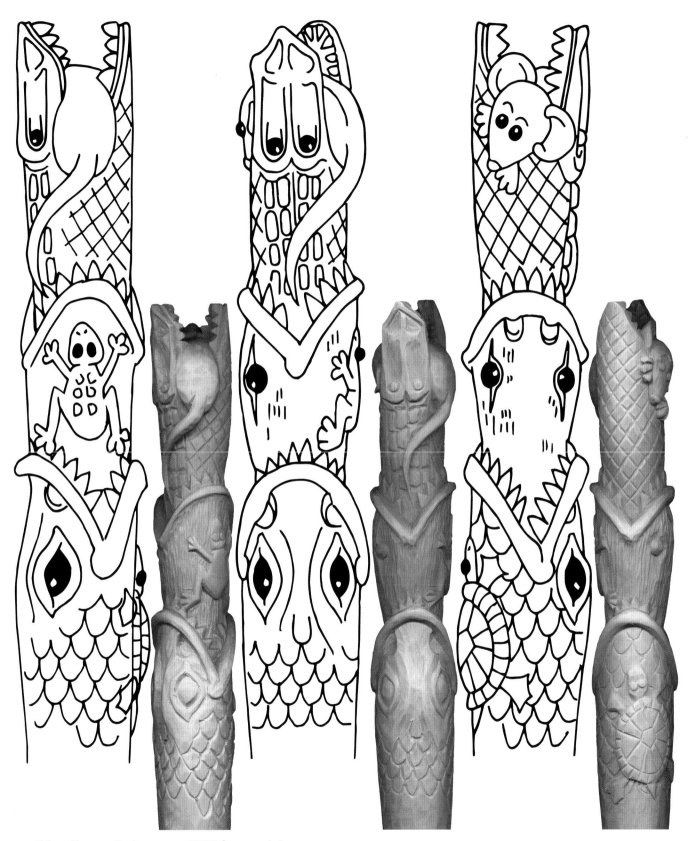

Critter Totem - Scale pattern 125% for actual size

Additional Patterns **165**

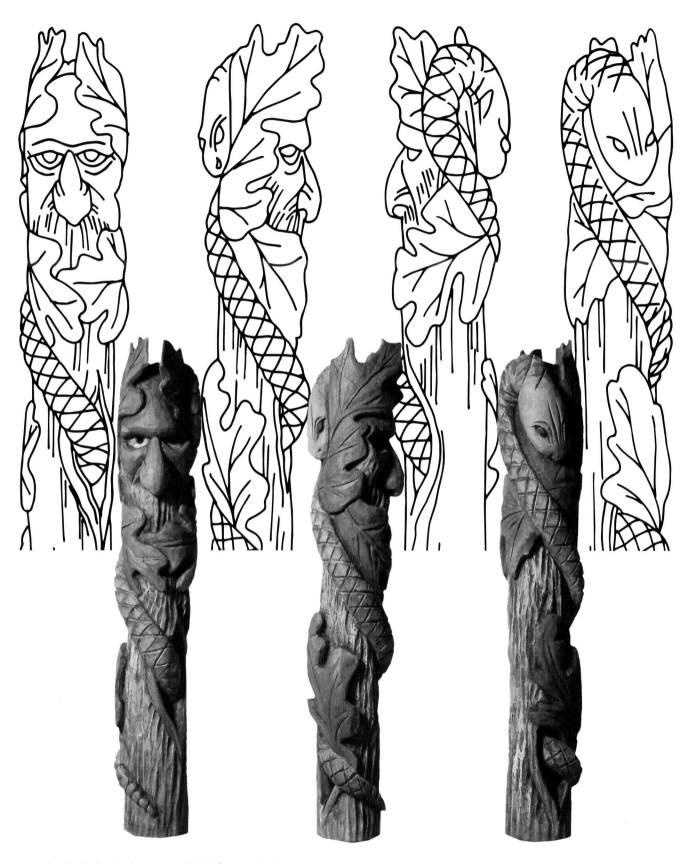

Snake Oak - Scale pattern 125% for actual size

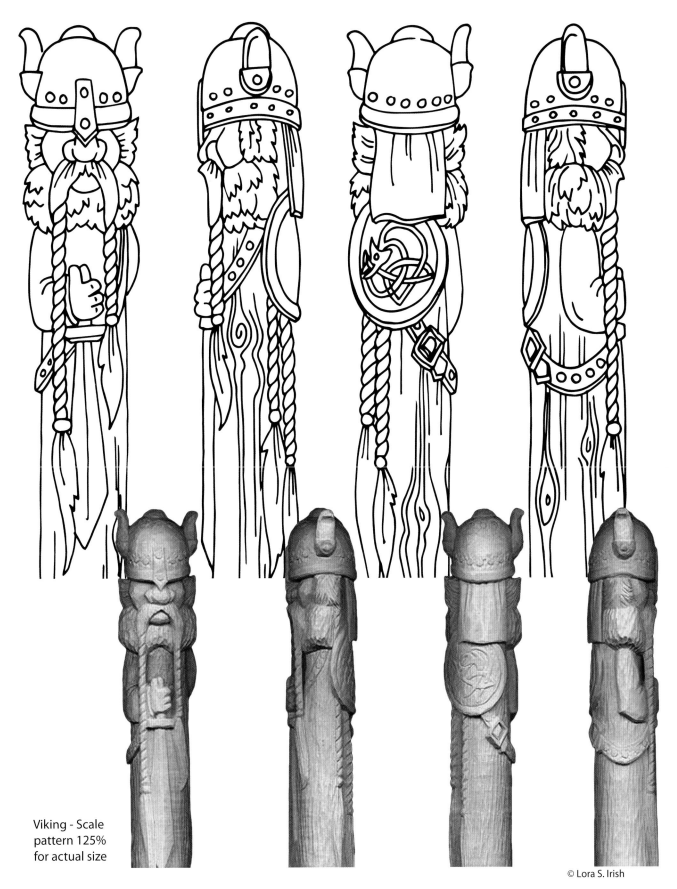

Viking - Scale
pattern 125%
for actual size

© Lora S. Irish

Wizard - Scale
pattern 125%
for actual size

© Lora S. Irish

Four Eagle Heads

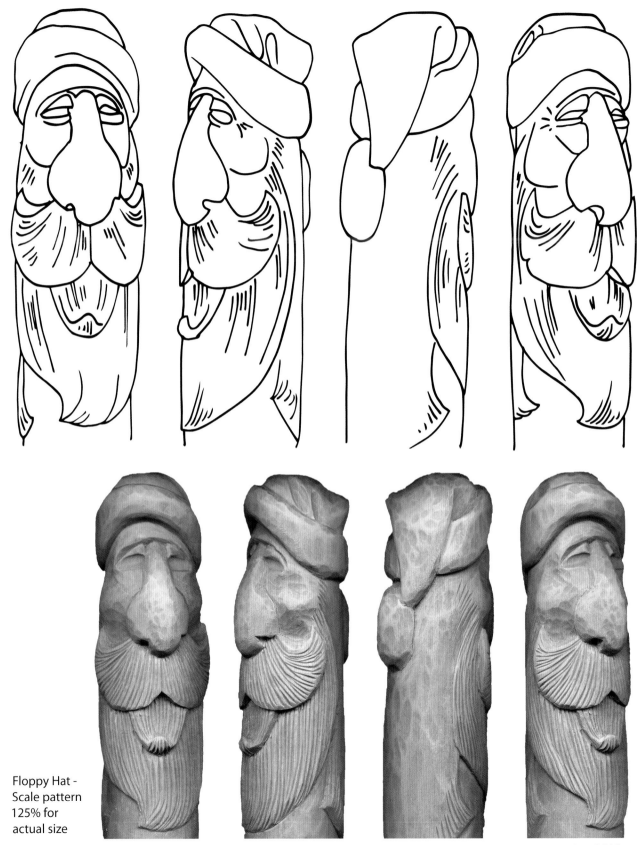

Floppy Hat -
Scale pattern
125% for
actual size

© Lora S. Irish

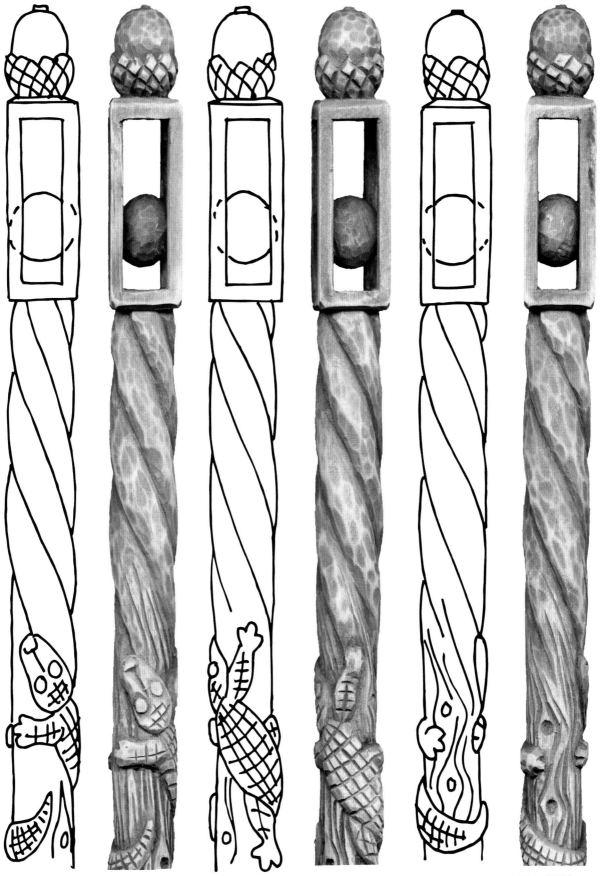

Ball in Cage

© Lora S. Irish

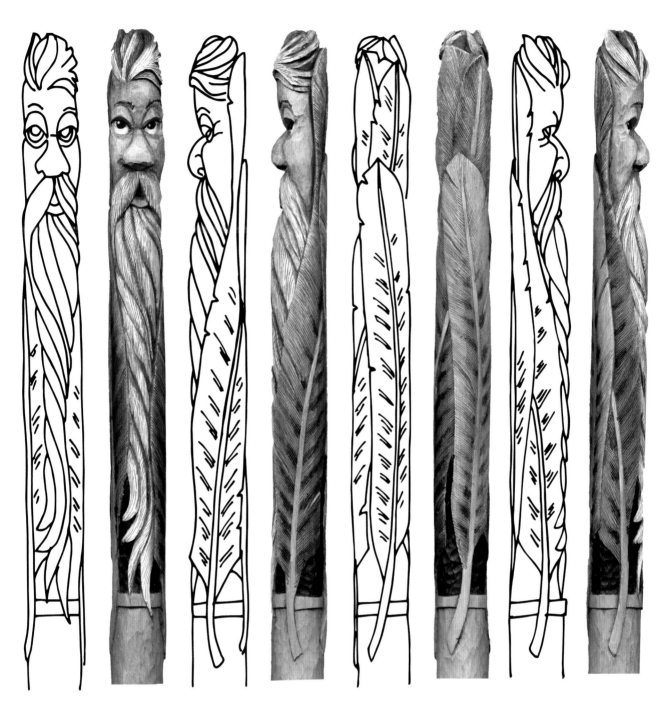

Feather Spirit - Scale pattern 125% for actual size

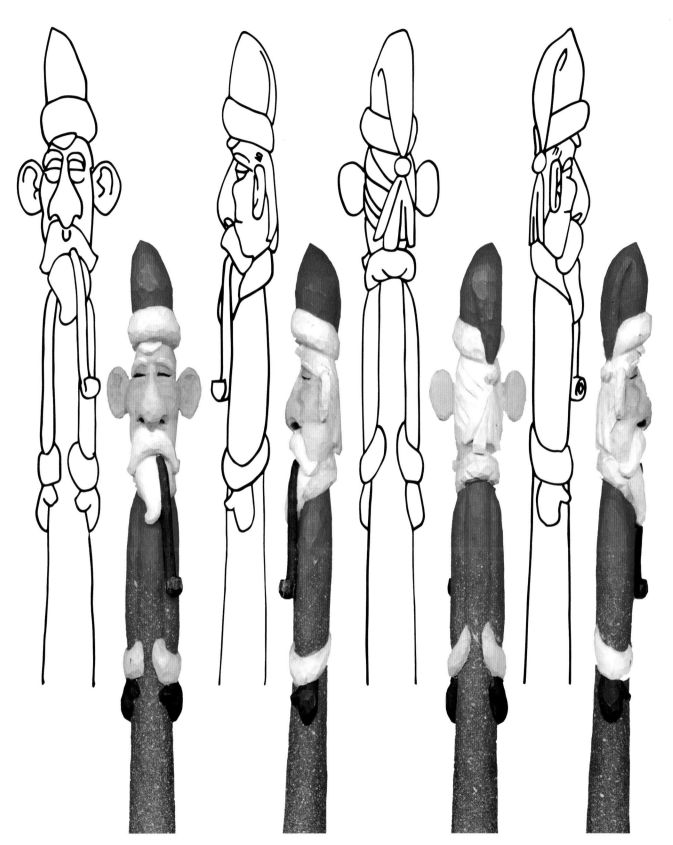

Smoking Santa - Scale pattern 125% for actual size

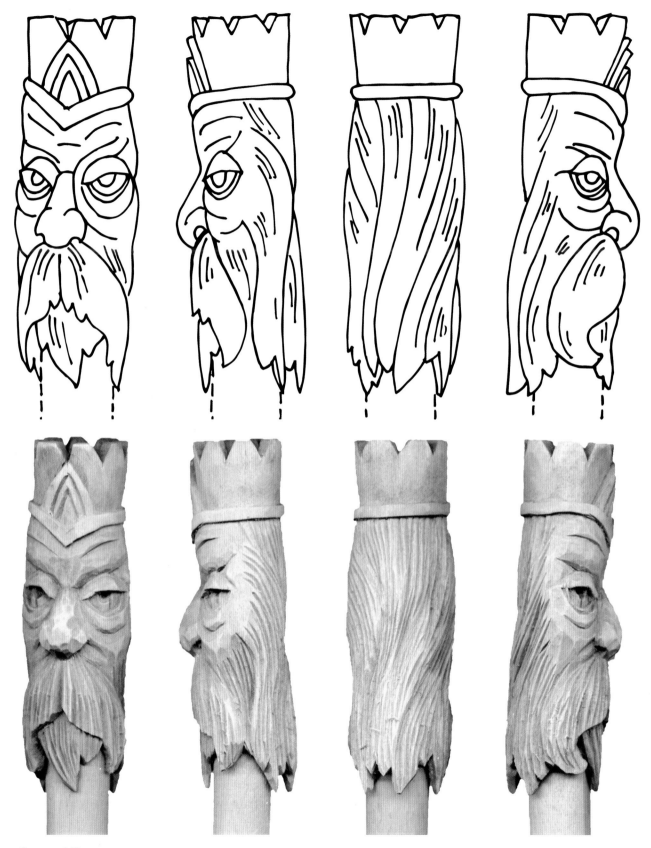

Crowned King

© Lora S. Irish

About the Author

Internationally known artist Lora S. Irish is the author of more than 30 woodcarving, pyrography, and craft pattern books.

Her books include *Great Book of Carving Patterns*, *World Wildlife Patterns for the Scroll Saw*, *The Art and Craft of Pyrography*, *Relief Carving the Wood Spirit*, *Great Book of Celtic Patterns*, and many more. Winner of the Woodcarver of the Year award, Lora is a frequent contributor to *Woodcarving Illustrated* and *Scroll Saw Woodworking & Crafts* magazines.

Working from her rural mid-Maryland home studio, she is currently exploring new crafts and hobbies, including wire jewelry, metal sheet jewelry, piece patch and appliqué quilting, gourd carving, gourd pyrography, and leather crafts. Visit her at *www.LSIrish.com*.

Index

Note: Page numbers in *italics* indicate projects and patterns.